dancing
in the
light

Meredith,
May you always
dance in the Light!.
Denise

Book design by The Troy Book Makers
Printed in the United States of America
The Troy Book Makers • Troy, New York • thetroybookmakers.com

ISBN: 978-1-61468-748-1

dancing

in the

light

*A Volunteer's Lessons in Faith
and Redemption in Africa*

Denise Stasik

introduction

About 15 years ago, I was engaged in a Bible study group discussion about being called to serve and what that means. One week, we delved into international humanitarian aid – how it can help and how it can hurt. I found it interesting that we were all intensely discussing it, but none of us had much real-life experience with the topic. Some expressed a feeling that as an individual, one could not affect any kind of sizable sustainable change. I disagreed with that, and I shared my experiences of volunteering in the Dominican Republic with people who seemed to be contributing to successful long-term projects related to educating the youth in rural communities.

I left the meeting feeling unsettled by that discussion. Something did not feel right, but I could not quite pinpoint what it was. That evening, as I read the local newspaper, I was drawn to a cartoon editorial depicting the continent of Africa. Ships from Turkey, Great Britain, and the United States were streaming by the West African shoreline on their way to provide much-needed relief to a Southeast Asian country that had been struck by a tsunami. All along the African coast, the cartoonist had drawn stick figures of women and children, each with their open hands stretched forth, requesting just a grain of rice from the supply-laden ships. The cartoon depicted the good-hearted humanitarian rush to contribute to recovery efforts when a natural disaster strikes. It simultaneously illustrated how it might be much easier to ignore, or "sail by," the day-to-day suffering that so many endure. Was I one of those people who had become numb and indifferent to this kind of daily suffering? That possibility troubled me.

I headed back to Bible study a week later. The discussion from the prior week continued, and in the end, we agreed to disagree on the topic of the effectiveness of small-scale international aid efforts. Feeling unsettled yet again, I drove home, prepared a cup of hot tea, and perused the local newspaper. My eyes were drawn to a photo of a child with the most enormous deep, dark eyes. I felt strangely connected to this child, as if she was beckoning me for some reason. The accompanying story was about a local nonprofit that was heading to Africa to work in a very remote village. My trip to the Dominican Republic had been a weeklong journey with people I had known for several years, and who spoke the country's official language. Was I ready to travel across the Atlantic to a new continent, to a place in which English was not the primary language, and with people who were strangers to me? Did I have a skill set that was needed there? Was I spiritually mature enough? Did I have enough personal funds to cover the overall costs of a trip like this? I decided to take the leap to find out, and with some trepidation, I called for more information.

I learned the nonprofit organization had traveled to this part of Africa several times and had established a strong relationship with the local leaders. As I heard more about village life and the needs of the people, I began to understand how I might be able to assist with some of the projects there while also learning from the villagers. Soon after, I volunteered to join the next traveling team.

Our team met several times prior to our departure to Africa. We learned about the travel logistics, cultural differences, anticipated language barriers, potential safety and medical issues, currency differences, day-to-day life in the villages, and our team's volunteer opportunities there. I enjoyed getting to know my teammates and hearing about their diverse backgrounds and experiences. I relished hearing stories about the people in the village who we would soon meet, and how they cohesively worked to weather the many challenges they regularly faced.

Random questions again flooded my mind. I wondered if I was up to the physical demands of traveling more than thirty hours each way on that journey. I wondered if my skills truly would be transferable to this African village. I wondered if I needed to worry about contracting malaria or cholera. I wondered if I would struggle with language barriers. At heart, I was still just a girl from a small coal-mining town in rural Pennsylvania. I wondered if that girl deserved a place on such an important mission. I wondered if this experience would change the way I looked at the world, and if I would embrace that change in me. But most of all, I was filled with the wonder that I was eagerly counting the days until we departed.

As our flight set its course from the United States to Africa, my doubts receded, replaced with gratitude for the gift of this special journey so far from home. Little did I know then that this was only the first step leading to many years of volunteering in Africa, and ultimately to sharing my experiences through this book to hopefully assist new volunteers in their own similar quests. But beyond that, my greater hope is to share with all readers, whether they are volunteer travelers or not, the wisdom and insight the people I encountered in Africa so graciously imparted to me. This evolved into a journey of faith for me, and that evolution brought me closer to God than ever before.

When you arrive in many African villages, a huge celebration awaits you. Women and children greet you in song and jubilant celebration. As I stepped out of our truck, I saw a little one running with determination, as fast as her tiny feet would carry her, directly towards me. When I scooped her up and our eyes met, I thought I recognized her as the same child whose picture was in the newspaper article. I carried that picture in my shirt pocket, and I quickly pulled it out and unfolded the paper. My assumption was confirmed when her teacher leaned near to see the clipping, and with great curiosity said, "Where did you get this child's picture?"

From that moment on, I knew where I was being called – not only to serve but even more so, to learn and to live out those lessons learned. Many new lessons awaited me. As the years progressed, I partnered with different not-for-profit organizations working in Africa for various lengths of time, including participating in short-term volunteer trips. Each experience gifted me with precious insight. Over time, those experiences culminated in a trifecta that I had long desired to achieve, that of my own physical, mental, and spiritual well-being all in balance (most of the time!).

After five years of volunteering in rural African villages, I heard an inner voice repeatedly saying, "Share your stories." I ignored it many times. My journal writings had always been for my eyes alone. I had not shared many of my experiences with larger groups of people, in part because I wondered if they would believe me, and in part because I needed time to process some of what I had seen and heard. The worrier in me thought, "What if my perceived experience was not the same as what someone else on our team had perceived?" And, "What if someone took my words out of context and made it into something that I had not intended?" My self-confidence and self-esteem were not yet strong enough.

As my volunteer trips to Africa continued, I began to realize that raising awareness and giving witness to what I have seen and heard there were responsibilities to embrace. I learned so much about culture, family, strength, faith, joy, trials, tribulation, and hope from the beautiful people I met in Africa. After more than a decade of volunteering, the Voice became more persistent: "Write your book."

Africa is a very large continent, with big cities, smaller towns, and remote villages. These stories capture the true events that I experienced in rural areas in several different east and south African countries. They are not in chronological order, but rather collated into sections reflecting the delightful joys, harsh realities, and practical advice related to short-term volunteering. The volunteering I describe is meant for those seeking assignments of less than six weeks, and for travel with or through an established not-for-profit organization which has achieved long-term success by working hand in hand with local African partners. Your own journeys and perceptions may differ from my mine, but the lifeline that runs through this type of experience will likely have many similarities.

But these stories are intended for a much broader audience, not exclusively for those who are interested in short-term volunteering. Any reader seeking true stories of human strength, resilience, perseverance, and spiritual awakening, can find those elements within the experiences that I share throughout the three sections of this book. Faith and hope in the face of adversity is a common thread that entwines many of us.

Poems written by children enrolled in an African village school are interspersed among the stories. I taught a poetry class to these students, aged eleven through fifteen. After reading poems by the likes of Browning, Nash, Frost, Longfellow, Dickinson, and others, I told the students to take twenty minutes to write any poems that spoke to whatever thoughts dwelled in their hearts. In that short period of time, and with no prior experience in reading or writing poetry, they drafted amazing works, with similar themes of hunger, AIDS, and mothers. Their words reflected their immediate needs, and often their understanding that they are part of a bigger cycle of life. As they read each poem out loud to the entire class, I could hear them express the sorrows and burdens that they carry. They agreed to allow me to share their poetry with others. May this sampling of their writings serve as a deeper insight to the children's everyday lives.

This book reflects experiences gained over more than a decade, and follows three major themes – Part 1 - Making a Difference: The Joys of Volunteering; Part 2 - Harsh Realities: Finding Hope in the Midst of Suffering, and Part 3 - Planning for Success: Practical Advice to Maximize Your Trip Experience. All three themes carry the same message I learned from the people I grew to know so well during these volunteer experiences – that in so many ways, we are all the same. When I use the phrase "we are all the same" in this context, I am referencing what I learned during my experiences of bonding with the women over our love and concern for our children and their future, sharing a meal together, joining in faith celebrations, discussing our health and other personal concerns, and expressing our laughter and joy together. I know that great disparities exist worldwide, and nothing that I share is meant to disparage or disrespect that. We may physically look different and have different life experiences. But within each of our life stories, we are all humans deserving of equal acknowledgement, respect and dignity, and we each deserve to belong in this world. And in this world, small acts of kindness matter.

The redemption I reference in this book's title is my own. For many years, I held myself captive with the inability to fully forgive and resolve hurts and disappointments borne over time. I felt that I was a faith-filled person, yet I knew that I did always not "walk by faith not by sight" (2 Corinthians 5:7). And I knew that I had not come close to being the person who I was created to be. Africa led me closer to understanding, and willingly embracing, the promise of redemption.

Africa and its amazing people have gifted me with many blessings. My hope is that I do justice in telling their stories.

PART I

Making a Difference: The Joys of Volunteering

We all have a baseline of knowledge and experience. I believed that my own baseline, which includes decades of living, had provided me with a broad view of the world. I was wrong.

Volunteering in Africa taught me to see beyond what was right in front of me. It taught me that joy has many faces, some that I had never before witnessed. Though I had believed my heart was already full, I learned that there was still so much room for growth.

The joys of volunteering in Africa come not from "giving back." The joy comes from listening and learning, and absorbing all that is good – the richness of its culture, the diversity of its people, the endurance of its traditions, and the beauty of its myriad landscapes. In doing so, your mind becomes deeply enriched, your knowledge expands and your heart opens wide to all that you see and hear. Your personal awareness of the gift of life blossoms as you encounter people who willingly impart their wisdom and life experiences. In the darkness of the African night, in its stillness, you may also feel an incredible sense of healing and peace.

You may head to Africa with a mission to "make a difference." And you may do just that. But Africa, in turn, will make a difference in your own life if you allow its joy to resound within your being. Tears of joy often streamed down my face as Africa touched my heart with a new lesson learned or a fresh experience revealed.

Volunteer with an open mind and welcome the joy that beats in the heart of Africa. The transformation within you can be an amazing multi-dimensional life experience. Be aware that Africa may very likely start to course through your veins, and the gravitational pull to return there never leaves you. The best part is that you grow to very much welcome that.

Gertrude

There was not a cloud in the sky, and the sun's rays continued to bake the hot sand outside of the village building in which we were holding a basic first-aid clinic. We prepared to visit the home of a young HIV/AIDS widow, who was also struggling with the manifestations of AIDS herself. She was unable to walk to the village to meet with us, and her friend requested that we make a hut call. As we prepared to make the eight-mile roundtrip walk in the scorching heat, one of our team members felt weak. She asked if we might be able to find transportation to the woman's home. Our team leader frowned on this suggestion, as everyone in the village walked these distances each day, and we were trying to establish strong community bonds, in part by following the community's norms ourselves. In addition, our van was already in use elsewhere. Walking was the only option. We headed toward the door.

At that moment, our African project manager, a native to the village, appeared in his van and offered to give us a ride. He had made other plans for the day, but due to unforeseen circumstances, a three-hour delay occurred. He had returned to see if he could be of any help to us. He agreed the weather was not conducive to the distance that needed to be traveled on foot, especially if we were not all in good health. Our team leader consented, and we loaded into the van.

When we arrived at our destination, we saw a small hut made of mud walls and a thatched roof. The air was so quiet and nothing was stirring. It seemed as if no one was home. Our project manager called out Gertrude's name. Gertrude had been resting on the dirt floor of her hut, and she responded to his greeting. She asked us to wait until she pulled herself upright to come outside and meet us. As we waited, our project manager explained that Gertrude's family had abandoned her and her children when they learned of Gertrude's HIV/AIDS status. Their fears were based on the lack of knowledge of how this virus is transmitted. She was all alone, desperately trying to care for her two young children.

Gertrude emerged, stick thin, slightly bent over from weakness, and barely able to walk. She had not eaten in a least a day, choosing instead to give her small amount of porridge to her children.

We shared with her the two loaves of bread, corn meal, rice, clothes, soap, washing powder, and medication. She began to kneel before us to pray and we moved to join her. Our project manager interpreted as Gertrude raised her hand in protest and said, "You have brought me many precious gifts for which I have prayed. Food for my children, soap to clean our bodies, and your love. Please, let me pray and give thanks for all that I have been given."

With that, Gertrude fell to her knees and raised her hands and face to the sky, and with a newfound strength in her voice, asked God to bless each of us, and to send wonderful gifts our way for the many precious blessings which she had just received. For that, we did not need an interpreter. All we had to do was gaze upon her face and hear the song of thanksgiving in her voice. It was the single most humbling moment of my entire life.

Before me, on her knees, was a young mother sincerely and fervently praying for us as if we had just given her millions of dollars. Tears streamed down our faces as she prayed. We asked if there was anything else that we could do for her personally. She showed us the soles of her feet, which were swollen and blistered. Through her broken English and with interpretative assistance by our project manager, she explained that when she fell ill, her formerly toughened feet had become very soft and sensitive, and that she felt like needles were piercing the skin of her feet. Walking barefoot on the hot sand was extremely painful.

I removed my new Teva sandals and put them on her feet. They were a perfect fit. She exchanged a piercingly loving look with me that I will never forget. With that, she made her way back to the hut to rest.

We drove back to the village in silence. When I stepped from the van, my bare feet burned within seconds of making contact with the hot sand.

I could take only a few steps, as the soles of my feet were already bright red. A teammate retrieved her extra pair of shoes from her backpack so that I could more easily make the short walk to the school building. As I cooled my feet, I realized that had we walked the four miles, it would have been very physically challenging for me to leave my shoes with Gertrude and make it back to the village. Yet another "coincidence" that our project manager's plans were unexpectedly delayed.

The next day, we prepared for a special event with the children. This was a schoolwide celebration with various foods provided by our team. Everyone would join in singing, dancing, and issuing student school awards. The children's parents were also invited to share in the celebration. As I walked toward the school classrooms to retrieve supplies, a woman tapped me on the shoulder. She smiled a radiant smile. Clearly she thought she knew me, but I did not recognize this beautiful woman standing before me.

The woman smiled with her own realization of my puzzlement, and she pointed down to her feet – and then I realized why she was now laughing. My sandals were strapped to her feet! When I looked up again, I recognized Gertrude's shining face. But today it was full of warmth and good health. She could walk. She could sing. She hugged me tightly. A teacher walking by stopped and interpreted for me.

Gertrude explained that yesterday she was so excited to prepare the food for her children as a surprise, and to wash them with soap, and clothe them with new garments. She began to feel a strength that she thought had long been lost within her. Gertrude professed that the sandals felt like a healing power on her feet. Indeed, the blisters were gone. Her children were being recognized at school that day as part of the special awards program, and in the past several months, she had been too weak to walk the four miles each way to see them participate in any school event. But today was different. "Today," she said, "I walk on angel's wings!"

Not a single word came from my mouth. How could that woman, so ill that she could barely stand, be the same person standing before me? Yet she was – with a twinkle in her eyes, a dance in her step, and the love of her children her day's mission.

And then she said this, "And if I am sick again tomorrow, I will always be thankful for this one day with my children. For today, I have no pain in my body or in my heart." With that, she gave me a quick hug and went off to surprise her children with her appearance at school. I knew the instant she found them, as shrieks of pure joy, mother and children together, filled the air.

Later that day, I offered her a ride home. She declined, stating that she preferred to walk and enjoy every moment of her blessing. Just then, a brightly colored bird flew overhead, tweeting a joyous melody. Gertrude paused and, with a gentle smile, turned her eyes upward toward the cloudless bright blue sky. And once again, as I watched her head home with a newfound peace in her heart and a temporarily pain-free body, I could taste the salt from my own tears. Gertrude will always be the angel who taught me how small acts of kindness can be transformed into something miraculous.

AIDS
(written by a girl, age 15)

AIDS, AIDS, AIDS
Oh my great danger,
The reaper of youth, parents, and school children.
Your journey to Uganda in 1982 was as silent as a grave,
Then the voices of orphans and widowers loudly arose,
Widows made me cry for their beloved ones,
 Your mass media was a stepping stone to fame.
AIDS, AIDS, AIDS
Where are you?
Where are your parents?
Where do you come from?
Who created you?
I wish I knew where you came from.
I would take you back from where you came.
You kill the young, you kill the old,
You kill the poor and you kill the rich.

AIDS – what is your problem??
You killed our grandparents,
You killed our parents, our brothers and sisters.
But I remain strong for God is the answer.
God is the only answer for me and my country.

Feast Day

On the day before our team's departure from a village in which we had spent two weeks doing volunteer work, a feast was held for all of the schoolchildren. On this celebratory day, the highs and lows of life here played out in several ways.

We asked the women if they would like to help with the cooking for the school-aged children. They not only wanted to help, they wanted to do it all! They were thrilled to have supplies such as salt, sugar, flour, and oil. These were all very rare commodities, as the cost of such items was prohibitive to people who earned less than one dollar a day.

The village women prepared dough and boiled biscuits in a pot of oil on an open fire. These were quite delicious. But the best-tasting biscuits I have ever eaten were prepared in a "convection oven." This was housed in a small hut. The oven consisted of a sand floor with a small fire burning, a layer of tin placed above the fire, the dough placed on the tin, another layer of tin above the dough, and a small fire atop that tin. The dough baked to a light, fluffy, and quite delicious biscuit.

The schoolchildren were so well mannered. They patiently waited in long lines to be served. The girls respectfully curtseyed and the boys bowed as they looked into your eyes and sincerely said "thank you" as they received their food. It was easy to get lost in the mixture of sadness and determination in their dark, piercing eyes.

I noticed a spindly-looking boy standing off to the side of the school. He did not join his grade's food line, even when encouraged to do so. I approached him and asked why he was not joining his friends. With a very factual accounting, he explained that this day of the week, Thursday, was not his day to eat. I did not understand so I asked what was different about Thursday. Continuing with a flat voice, he said, "My family has little food," and he counted on his fingers, "So I eat on Monday, Wednesday, and Friday. Today is Thursday. It is not my day to eat."

He said this not with sadness, just with acceptance. As I gazed at this beautiful, thin child, my heart hurt with the realization of what he was explaining to me. It simply was not his day to eat. And as such, he did not want to deprive someone else of his or her day to eat.

I sat beside him in the sand and explained we had food for everyone. This was a day to celebrate our friendships and as my new friend, would he do me the honor of joining in this celebration? I assured him that all of the children would have food on this day. With hesitancy, he agreed. My heart still hurt for him.

(As an aside, when I first retold this story to a college student body audience back home, one of my teammates suggested I not state that some children go an entire day or two without eating. He explained many people in the United States may not believe that. As I looked around the auditorium, I realized he was right. Not one person there absorbed that children in this world truly do go for a day or more with absolutely no food. It might be easier to assume that I had exaggerated than to genuinely accept this unsettling truth.)

As I jumped back into the food serving line, I noticed several plates full of food just sitting in the sand. Where had the children gone? I looked up and saw them returning from the bush (the remote parts of the village), each toting a younger brother and sister. This was a school event, so the younger siblings were at home. When the school-aged children realized that on this special day they were being provided with an abundant plate of food, they rushed home to gather their younger siblings – before taking even one bite from their plates themselves.

I watched one little boy return to his spot with a brother and sister on each hip. All were bone thin, but perky and smiling. This boy encouraged each of them to eat until they were full. Then he took his own first bite of food. As I turned, I saw the same scenario play out in other families. Instead of consuming all that was before them, their first instinct was to share it with their siblings.

One boy was sharing his plate with three younger family members. Only a very minimal amount of food remained for his consumption. I joined them and offered an additional plate of food. He looked up and with a maturity unlike any that I have ever witnessed, said, "Thank you, but this is plenty for my family. Please give that to someone else who has not eaten today and is hungry." Again, yet another speechless and emotional moment for me. I looked at him and he looked at me with a gaze that conveyed his sincerity and command of the situation. Such strength and control from such a little boy. He had become the teacher, and I, his student. I walked away with the plate of food still in my hands. My head knew it was the right thing to do, but once again, my heart hurt.

The older children at the secondary school joined us for this Feast Day. They asked us to change the order of the food distribution, requesting to move the biscuits to the first station instead of the last. One look at their dishes explained the reason for this, as their bowls were mostly cracked pieces of plastic, which the students desperately tried to hold together with their hands. Without the bread as the base, the beef broth and gravy ran right through the dish and onto the ground. These children did not want to waste one bit of food.

As the line of children to be served dwindled, we realized we would have some food remaining. Deciding to whom that would be served rested with the village elders. Cultural tradition dictated the pregnant women would be served next, then the men. Then, if the food supply was not exhausted, the remaining women would eat.

At this point, I noticed such an endearing act on the part of the married men. In this culture, the men played a domineering role as far as decision-making and position within the village. Yet these men realized that the food supply would likely run out before their wives would be served. I watched as they quietly reserved half of their food portion should that happen. And when it did happen, these men just as quietly motioned to their wives to join them in sharing the remaining portion of food. I witnessed discreet glances of love exchanged among these couples. And their children witnessed this too. And they smiled. Love of family is universal and it is such a powerful, protective embracing bond.

<u>Strength of Love</u>
(written by a girl, age 13)

Love is found everywhere in Africa, Asia, America, Europe,
Love is not determined by the mind, head, or brain,
But it is determined by heart.
Love is something one should treasure.
For life is incomplete without a love.
Love gives meaning to people who are helpless, like orphans.
Love has the greatest power. It heals.

Alfred

The day before departing Africa to head back to the United States one year, I sat on the rocks in the village schoolyard, trying to absorb all that I had experienced on this amazing trip.

Several rows of rocks of varying sizes were lined up neatly between the two school buildings. One large white rock was positioned at the forefront of these rows. I thought they were the remnants of children's play. One of the teachers explained that seldom do her students have the luxury of owning a pencil and even less often a piece of paper. I recalled that when we previously provided these supplies to the children, their writing was so small, never wasting any space on each side of that one sheet of paper, and they took three days to fill both sides with their lessons.

The rocks in the schoolyard were used when no writing utensils were available. Each child perched on one of the rocks, in full sun, and the teacher stood at the head of these rows, instructing her students in math and writing skills. The students practiced their lessons by using sticks to write in the dirt at their feet.

I thought of the number of times that I began to write on a sheet of paper, did not like how my draft looked, and crumpled that paper and started with a fresh one. And how many pencils had I thrown away because they were not sharp enough and I was too lazy to sharpen them? I thought about how earlier in the week I had been working in the first-aid clinic and I needed to write a reminder to myself about medical supplies and patient follow-up treatment plans. I reached into my backpack only to find it empty, and then remembering that I had left my notebook at our place of lodging. I set out to find a piece of paper – just one piece would do. I searched the classrooms, in all of the other buildings, in the teacher's quarters. There was not one sheet of paper to be found. What an odd feeling, that with all of paper in the world, some places had not even a single sheet on which to make notes. Eventually I settled on inking my skirt with the notes, and I gained a whole new appreciation for a full ream of paper.

Turning my attention to tomorrow's departure, I began to inventory my clothes to determine what I wanted to leave for the villagers' use. Most of my clothes were new, purchased specifically for this trip, so that I would be dressed in accordance with the village culture. I knew I would be returning, so I did not want to purchase many replacement garments.

As I reflected on that, I saw my young friend Alfred walking down the path from his hut. This year nine-year-old boy had assisted me many times during my stay in the village. Wearing a shirt so ragged that it was more holes than cloth, Alfred was always smiling. He never asked for anything in return. Two days prior, I had offered him a new shirt and he chose a bright yellow, extra-large T-shirt that would fit him for years. With a big grin, he ran home wearing his new shirt, carrying the ragged one under his arm.

Yet here he was wearing the old shredded rag. And there was his much older, taller neighbor, wearing the yellow shirt. I knew what had happened!

So I beckoned to Alfred to come and sit with me. He eagerly ran over and greeted me with his bright smile. I asked him where his new yellow shirt might be. He pointed to his friend, Maguri. Just as I was about to give him a lesson in letting others take advantage of him, he leaned forward and excitedly whispered, "Maguri is so smart. Really smart. He could be president of us one day. He cannot go to school every day because he has no shirt to wear. His brothers have a shirt and they take turns wearing it to school. So Maguri can only go to school one day or maybe two days every week."

Alfred excitedly continued, "So I said to myself, 'Alfred, give him your big yellow shirt. You have two shirts and he needs one.' And now Maguri can go to school every day. We are all happy."

With that, Alfred ran off to join the other boys. I heard them good-naturedly tease him about the special attention that I had paid to him, and his laughter filled the air with the sound of a young boy happy to be playing netball with his friends.

I sat there, reflecting even more deeply. How could I be so wrong, so judgmental? Then I looked up to the sky and softly said, "OK, God, I finally get it. I am supposed to leave ALL of my clothes here when I go back home." And I willingly did just that.

Alfred exemplified the literal meaning of "giving the shirt off of his back." For he was sincerely happy clothed in rags, knowing that his new shirt was the vehicle to make another's dream come true. I think of Alfred's selflessness often, especially when I allow material things to become more important than those gifts in life which cannot be purchased.

When you are volunteering in a village, take the time to get to know the children who live there. They are amazing teachers.

Am Beautiful
(written by a girl, age 14)

Short people admire tall people, and the inverse is true.
The dark skinned admire the light skinned,
    yet the light skinned also feel out of place.
Those in the desert are tall and thin,
    while those in the winter are short and fat.
The blind love to see, the deaf love to hear.
The crippled love to walk, but the lazy hate to work.
Am blessed to be loved and to have all that I have,
To be just who I am,
Am Beautiful.

Loaves and Fish

Our team embarked on another trip to rural Africa, arriving late afternoon on a weekday. We decided to make the hour-long drive to the village project site to orient ourselves. We first stopped by the city store to purchase juice and biscuits for any children who might be playing near the schoolyard. While the biscuits were plentiful in supply, only a few plastic cups and three bottles of concentrated juice mix were available for purchase. We would usually purchase about nine bottles to serve drinks to all of the village children. We thought this would not be a problem since school was recessed for the day and most of the children were already back at their homes.

Upon arriving at the village, we invited the twenty or so children who were still playing in the schoolyard to join us for a snack. As we prepared the juice, the children eagerly lined up in front of the school building's window. My teammate and I began filling the plastic cups with juice and handing them to the children.

After distributing about ten cups of juice, I noticed that the line of children had become longer. Then it got longer, and even longer. As word spread that we had arrived, very thirsty and hungry children came streaming from the bush. The children stood in a seemingly endless line and were very orderly and polite, while I began to feel anxious about our minimal supplies.

From the back of the room I heard our team leader call for us to start to distribute half cups of juice. Shortly thereafter, she called out for quarter cups of juice to be poured. But even if we did so, we would never have enough for the number of children now in line.

The children approached our distribution window with a multitude of drinking vessels. Some were old oil cans, with the dirty brown oil still adhering to the inside of the cans. Others were cracked plastic bottles and barely capable of holding any amount of fluid. Some were hollowed-out tree roots.

One boy held out a water bottle, had his drink, and then passed it back to his brother who was further down the line. His brother did the same for their other brother, who was waiting even further back in the queue. I saw this same water bottle four times that day. What was significant about this particular water bottle is that it bore the logo of my employer in the United States. And it was the company's brand new logo. No one on the team had carried it there and to this day, it remains a mystery of how that bottle made its way to this remote African village. I found myself mindlessly and repeatedly pouring more juice into this water bottle than I was pouring into the rest of the containers. Later, I was struck by how easily I favored the familiar, allotting greater distribution to the container to which I could personally relate, instead of sharing equally to each and every container. It was a good lesson for any volunteer, and especially me, to ponder.

One team member ran to the well to fill a bucket with water to wash the oil and dirt from the cans and plastic bottles before we added any juice. He made his way down the line of children who were patiently waiting their turn. The line seemed to be getting longer.

A few minutes later, I glanced out the distribution window again. The queue of children still waiting seemed even longer. I was not yet experienced in a situation like this. Panic suddenly engulfed me as I realized for certain that we could not possibly provide drinks for all of these children. "What are we going to do here?" I asked, "We can't give this to some of the children then tell the others to just go home."

My teammate smiled and very calmly said, "How about if I just take care of pouring the juice and you just keep handing it out?" Meanwhile from the back of the room I again heard reminders to start pouring less than quarter cups.

My eye rolls were directed towards my teammate as I replied, "Are you talking like loaves and fish?" She smiled and calmly said, "Something like that."

And so we pressed on, she poured full cups of juice and I handed them out. At the end of the day, all of the children had a cup of juice and several biscuits. Their happy voices resounded as they ran home. I looked over at the juice bucket and saw that we had about two cups left. A sigh of happy relief escaped my lips.

The true miracle of this did not strike me until the next day. We were able to purchase additional supplies in the city before we headed back to the village school. We prepared the same juice for these same children.

This time, the same quantity was poured into the cups, yet it took three times as many bottles of juice to serve these children.

The school's senior teacher had been helping us during the prior day's juice distribution, so I went to find her. I asked if she had further diluted the juice the day before. She said, "No, but I was not for certain that the supply would be enough for all children." When she realized that the juice supply was running very low, she went to see if there were more bottles in our truck. Finding none, she returned and saw that the pails of juice were replenished, so she just assumed that I had mixed more from new bottles that I might have carried in earlier, or that I had just added more water.

Realizing that neither of us diluted the juice, she patted my shoulder and said, "Don't question. Just accept." Often that can be good advice to a short-term volunteer. Sometimes you just need to trust in things that cannot be seen or otherwise explained. The more I learned to do that, the more sense things actually made to me – and I learned to stop rolling my eyes so much.

<u>Untitled</u>
(written by a boy, age 11)

God, I am a very special creature,
I have wings, hands and legs.
Look into the Bible to know more about me,
I am an angel.
Created to be God's messenger,
Look into your Bible to learn more about me in your church.
Amen.

Priscilla

In one village, I became attached to a young girl named Priscilla. At first, a few members of our team affectionately, and perhaps in hindsight inappropriately, referred to her as "The Hustler." This nine-year-old girl had a different sad story every day and constantly practiced her facial expressions of different emotions as she tried to hustle watches, jewelry, and shoes from our team members. She could look incredibly grief-stricken and softly state, "I have no mother. My mother is dead. My father is dead, too. I have nowhere to live. I have nothing to eat." Other times she would ask for material things, boldly and with firm vocal command, stating, "I am all alone. I am an orphan. I have nothing. What can you give me to live?" She even demonstrated how she could make herself cry on demand – the best crocodile tears that I had ever seen. It was all part of her survival skills. It was the only way she knew to secure basic needs. At such a young age, she understood the language of what would deeply affect the hearts of those who may come into her life for brief moments in time. And she knew that older men paid attention to her.

A woman from the village shared that this girl's mother died slowly and painfully of HIV/AIDS a few years ago at the family's home, and that the girl now lived with her father, who was often at work. This little girl was responsible for her younger sister, who spoke infrequently, but was always clinging to her older sister's side, as if her sister had assumed the role of mother. Priscilla had seen much pain, loneliness, and sorrow in her young life.

I made a deal with her that if she practiced telling me the truth about her life rather than trying to make us believe the many stories that she so easily fabricated, I would make time each day to just sit and talk with her. Priscilla talked about the deep loss and loneliness that she felt with her mother gone, the worry of caring for her sister, the lack of a regular adequate food supply for her family, and most of all, her fear of not knowing who she really is or if anyone actually loves her. At nine years of age, she had become so good at conning people for food or small amounts of money or trinkets that she wondered if she was already living all that her future would ever bring. Her stories started to have the feel of truth. At times, that made her uncomfortable, for she was not accustomed to sharing what resided deep in her heart.

I spent much time with her and taught her songs like "I Am Special" to remind her that she truly is special, just her with her beautiful face and big brown eyes, without all of the hustling. I was teaching her the song "This Little Light of Mine," when she smiled and joined in singing the chorus, telling me that she knew this song from her church. She looked up and asked me when it would be her turn to shine her light.

I often do not reveal much about my personal life with the children, but I shared this story with her.

When I was very young, I was frequently chased by a vicious little white dog whose owners just let it run wild. One day when I was walking home from where the school bus dropped me off each day, this fiercely snarling animal ran full force straight towards me. I ran, but not fast enough this time, and the dog tore my socks and sunk his teeth into my skinny legs in several spots. The local doctor gave me painful shots in each of my bony hips. I could not walk for three days. I was so traumatized by that and by just lying in bed waiting for the bites to heal and the pain to subside, that I could not – would not – talk to anyone.

An older gentleman came to our house unannounced and brought me a hand-carved butterfly. He asked me if I knew the story of the butterfly and, without waiting for my reply, proceeded to tell me how it starts out as a caterpillar, slowly crawling on the ground, trying its best to not get stepped on, and then one day it just rolls itself up in a blanket and rests for a while. He said that takes a lot of patience. In time, it emerges from the blanket, and flies away with its new wings and new confidence. He said it is a thing of beauty. Then he told me that I too had to be patient because right now I was a caterpillar. But with rest and faith and patience, I would become a butterfly, and walk and take flight again. And then he left me with a small carved butterfly.

I fell asleep, and when my father came to check on me, I told him about this man. He said that no one else had been there, that he was at home the entire time. Yet there I was, holding this little butterfly. He said that one of the neighbors must have stopped by when he stepped outside to smoke a cigarette.

I treasured this butterfly because that analogy, even in my little girl's mind, was enough for me to break through the fear and pain that was gripping me. I continued to heal. Even now, my heart sometimes still skips a beat whenever I hear a dog barking, especially when I am walking or bicycle riding, but that fear is greatly diminished. In time, I passed that butterfly on to someone else who needed to hear that story, and he passed it on to someone else, and as far as I know, it is still being passed on as the receiver heals and encounters someone else who needs healing. While I no longer know where that butterfly rests, I am certain that it continues to remind people in pain or in fear of their inner beauty waiting to emerge.

I told Priscilla that maybe sometimes we are like the caterpillar just trudging along, practicing patience, trying to not get stepped on, learning life's lessons as we crawl through our days. And then maybe sometimes, when the time is right, we become like the butterfly, with new wings, floating deftly and gracefully through the day, with confidence, making people smile with our unique beauty and grace.

Priscilla smiled and said, "It's like me, the caterpillar and the butterfly. When I am afraid or frustrated, I act like a woman without first learning to be a girl."

In the end, I was the one who learned so much from this bright and observant little girl. She shared with me what life was like foraging for food, walking long distances carrying heavy water containers, not being able to attend school every day, having men stare at her and not knowing who to trust, being afraid to close her eyes at night because tomorrow might not be a better day. She showed me the large rocks that marked the graves of her two close friends, both of whom had died of HIV/AIDS complications. She cried, real tears this time, as she described their pain and frailty. She kept our bargain and at the end of the week, and after receiving permission from our African project manager, she was wearing my shoes, the ones she had tried to hustle from me on the day we first met, as recognition for her honesty. She smiled with joy and said, "Today I shall be a butterfly. I can tell the truth – and people still like me!"

We continued to talk and Priscilla began to slowly but increasingly value herself for who she really was. We again sang "I Am Special," a song that she referred to as "her song." When I returned a year later, she had grown taller and more confident in herself. As we walked holding hands, she asked me if I remembered her song, and she sang it for me. Then she looked up at me and said, "Denise, I love you with all of my heart for teaching me that people will love me just for being myself."

My heart grew in that very second as tears filled my eyes. The small nonmaterial things that any of us can do have the power to make a positive difference in the life of a child. And that, in turn, makes a positive difference in our own lives.

I worry about Priscilla always, so young and so alone in such a grown-up role. There are millions of beautiful children just like her. My hope is that they be given time to be the caterpillar, to feel the warmth of the cocoon, then when the time is right, to burst forth and spread their wings and soar.

Years later, I was volunteering on an African island and I was working with a young woman who coordinated her own nonprofit's work there. This young lady was stunningly beautiful in every way. She had a large delicate butterfly tattooed on the side of her abdomen. The words "Life is not always easy, but our wings get stronger" were tattooed below the butterfly. She shared that these were her father's words of advice to her as she pursued her own adventurous journey in life, and that they were written in his own handwriting.

Life is not always easy. The more you experience on your volunteer trips, the stronger your wings will grow.

Some Day, Some Way
(written by a girl, age 13)

Some day you will be able to achieve your dreams,
For everything has a beginning and an end,
Those who trust in themselves are like Mount Zion,
Which does not move, eat or drink, but lasts forever.
Don't lose hope,
Some way you will make it.
Crops, plants, animals don't plan for themselves,
But they don't lose hope – they survive.
Some day, Some way.
Hope and believe in yourself.

We Are All the Same

I was demonstrating how to make animal figures using the shadows of my hands cast against the classroom wall. The children and I practiced making a bird in flight, a camel's head, a butterfly, a rabbit, a goat, and an elephant. As I watched the children artistically explore their own shadow creations, one little girl, graced with beautiful, almond-shaped, deep brown eyes, held her hand up and pressed her palm firmly against my own. Pointing to the back of my hand, she said, "Your hand is so white." I smiled and replied, "Yes, it is." Then she pointed to her own hand and said, "And my hand is so black." Again I acknowledged that she was correct. Then she rotated her hand outward so that our palms aligned side by side with each other. Peering over the tips of our fingers, at our palms which were varying shades of light color and quite similar, she exclaimed, "But on the inside we are the same!"

Could this little one possibly understand the magnitude of her observation? Such wisdom from the mouth of a babe. We may look different in some ways on the outside, but inside we truly are all the same.

She continued to count the fingers on our respective hands, announcing that they were equal in number, or as she said, "They count to the same!" From that moment on, her observation became my mantra: We are all the same. We all need assistance of some kind during our lives. If we look down on someone who has fallen, it should be only to extend our own hand down to help him or her back up. I have seen so many people who are in great need, and under the right circumstances, any of us could easily be one of them. There have been times when I was actually the one in need of help up when I have fallen. I remain determined to always remember that and to promote this mantra: We are all the same. And we are here to help each other.

Volunteering can create a gamut of emotions in most people. When I deeply immersed myself in African culture, I suddenly felt my heart swell with love. My spirituality reached heights I did not think I could achieve. And my understanding that "We are all the same" became forefront in my thinking.

I saw children laughing and playing and overjoyed to see our team arrive. I carried around three children at a time. Never did I have a free hand, for my hands were always tightly woven to those of several little ones. I sang songs, not caring what my voice sounds like. I sat in a village worship service for several hours and was drawn in by the incredible singing and dancing and deep faith of the Africans. I saw this to also be true for people on the team who had not attended church services in many years. A random child would rest in my lap, and I could just feel her body relax in the peace of the moment. And I too felt that peace. Sometimes it took me by surprise, that moment of just being in the moment, of being still.

I also heard the cries of pain in these children and women, knowing that they have no access to medical care. And I cried too. And then I cried more later. I saw six-year-old children who were now playing the role of parents to their younger siblings. I saw them walk all day in the hot sun carrying their brother or sister on their tiny backs. I watched the children struggle to hand pump water from the well, and then carry these very heavy loads back to their homes, repeating that several times a day. I heard the children's coughs from tuberculosis and felt the heat from their fevers from malaria. I saw a small bowl of rice or a single small guinea hen that would be the entire meal for a family of five that evening. I heard the children tell you that even though they cannot go to school, they yearn to be doctors and nurses and teachers in their country one day. I wanted to give them hope. I saw the tiny grave markers where children who had no hope are buried. And I cried some more.

Yet very often in these villages I saw someone in need, someone with seemingly nothing, give whatever they have to someone else in greater need. I have also seen them present their day's food ration, a live chicken, coconuts, mangos or papayas, and sometimes the last of their coins, in reverent and deep appreciation to volunteers.

When we attended a morning mass at a rural village church, the local community did not know that our team was joining the services until the evening before. During mass, they joyously took up a collection of all of their coins and presented it to us in a basket, stating that if they had time to prepare for our visit they would have served a lunch for us. Instead they requested that we accept their monetary offering to buy chicken and sodas for our lunch later that day. We had an extremely difficult time accepting this, for it was an enormous sacrifice for them to make. But they insisted, and refusing their abundant generosity would have been quite rude and disrespectful. So with mixed emotions, we accepted their heartfelt generosity, as their voices raised in the song of "When He calls me, I will answer. I'll be somewhere working for my Lord."

After mass, we all gathered in the churchyard, and I spoke with the presiding minister, again expressing our uneasiness with this extremely generous gift. He reminded me that this gift was given with deep sincerity and could not be refused. He said, "Gifts from the heart are meant to be given away." He then told me to read Hebrews 6:10, as he pointed in the direction of the church. So I went back into the church and opened a Bible that was lying near the altar. Hebrews 6:10: "God is not unjust; he will not forget your work and the love you have shown him as you have helped his people and continue to help them." While recognition and reward are things I hope to never seek, if my volunteer hands can be a vehicle for helping others, then I needed to learn to be more comfortable receiving these gifts from the heart.

Often villagers will invite you to attend their Sunday worship celebrations. Regardless of your faith or beliefs, join them. Scoop up that small child who meanders over to rest on your lap. These are special experiences not to be missed.

Love!
(written by a girl, age 13)

Love! Love !Love!
It makes you laugh, and later makes you cry.
It strengthens you in times of trouble,
     but can weaken you in the knees and soul.
It values no tribe, levels, and race, but it gives hope and encouragement.
Love makes one forget about the past and concentrate on the present,
Predicting the future.
Man can't live without love,

Because it is the beginning of everything that is started in the world.
You really want to know it!
Some days I try to ask questions about love, but I fail to get answers,
Cause love has so many definitions and meanings.
So go and find your answer – and love!

The Elder Woman

Our team met with village women who had formed a sewing and knitting club. Their organization was impressive. They proudly displayed their notebook with meeting minutes, complete with goals and tracking of each item that was ready for sale.

We spent hours talking with them, just being girls. I reveled in their spirit and strength. They shared stories about everyday life that mimicked what we had heard in other villages. They described searching for food, sometimes walking ten miles each way for a free government ration of three cups of cooking oil, two cups of rice, and some porridge. They described a daily routine of rising at daybreak to walk a long distance for water, carrying five gallons of water on their heads back to their homes, then making an open fire from wood and dry leaves so they could boil the water. No breakfast would be served, but with some green leaves plucked from the field to add color to hot water, their young daughters would feel as if they had some hot tea in their hungry bellies before starting off on the long walk to school.

These women talked about losing newborn babies who became afflicted with severe diarrhea from the contaminated water. Babies and children continued to die of malaria. Who could afford the six dollars for the treatment when a day's wage is less than one dollar? When no rains came, severe dehydration and malnutrition resulting from the extensive drought conditions took the lives of even more children. I thought, "How in this world can children be dying because they have no water? No water at all?" I was still very naive in my volunteer experiences. The women's depictions left no doubt that this is a horrible way to die. And what deep, unending pain these young mothers then endure.

As time went on, I refocused and looked more closely at these women as they spoke. Their faces were lined with deep wrinkles. Their skin was leathery, so dry and so rough. Their lips were cracked and parched. The palms of their hands and the soles of their feet bore thick callouses. Yet their eyes twinkled with the joy of creating this bond with us. Their natural broad smiles made me smile, even when I did not understand the dialect spoken by some. I did not need to know the exact words, for in that laughter and animated storytelling, I knew what was being expressed. Being part of this bonding was making my wings grow stronger.

Our team members asked if they could purchase the handmade items the women had on display and they eagerly agreed. We continued to bond and strengthen our connections to each other. I spoke about the beauty I saw in each of these women. As we concluded our purchases of the entire stock of their exquisite handmade goods, the oldest village woman stood up to speak. Now this woman was greatly respected by all. She seldom spoke. Her role was to patiently listen, and to speak when speaking really mattered. When she did speak, her words ruled.

Big tears welled in her deep brown eyes. She threw her head back and closed her eyes. I watched her tears caress the wrinkles on her face. They flowed softly and gently down her cheeks. And raising her hands and face to the blue cloudless sky, she said, "Thanks be to Jesus. For from this day forward, I will no longer allow anyone to call us useless people. We are children of God, and He has sent people to us to let us know that truth." Her tears poured forth even faster. Her inner spirit glowed, and her eyes shined with new hope and commitment. Her trembling hands seemed to reach for the heavens.

I asked her what she meant: what was a useless person? She said she has often heard visitors, as well as people in her own country from opposing tribes, use that term when addressing her and the other women in the village. She said, "It means that we were born to die. Born ONLY to die, nothing more. We are useless because there is no hope for our kind."

Born only to die. I tried to absorb that thought. Could I ever imagine being called a useless person because I had no material possessions? Or because of where I was born? Sitting among this circle of strong women was such a great privilege. Their minds were keen. Their experiences of survival and love were unlike any I had ever heard. Their commitment to their families was unwavering. They were beautiful beings. Never would the word "useless" enter my mind as I sat among them, wrapping myself in their presence, with such great respect for each of them. I offered silent abundant thanks for the gift of being part of this circle of women.

Competing questions rapidly flooded my mind. Why do we sometimes allow material possessions to master us? Why do we sometimes judge a person's worth based on those material possessions? Why is it sometimes difficult to reach out to offer someone direct heartfelt assistance? Why is it easier to look away and ignore? Should where a person is born be the major determinant of whether they live or die? Am I helping or hindering? Was I doing enough to share my own blessings with others? How do I help these women? Am I even asking the right questions?

I rejoiced as I listened to this woman speak of breaking the chains of a "useless person," setting herself free, and asserting her right to be part of humanity. I prayed that one day I would fully develop even just a smidgeon of her courage and conviction.

A Poem
(written by a boy, age 12)

I wrote my name in a book,
    but the book got lost,
I wrote my name on the road,
    but the wind came with dust and rubbed it away.
I decided to write it on a stone,
    but the heavy rains washed it away.
I decided to write it high on a tree leaf,
    but a bird came and picked it away,
Then I decided to write it in my heart,
Where nobody can disrupt my name.

Curing Cataracts

A weak knock sounded at the wooden door to our team's small medical clinic in the village. An elderly man timidly entered the room, asking for help with his vision. "I have cataracts," he said, "Can you please take them out?"

I looked into his eyes and did not see the more typical lens cloudiness that I had observed in some of the other men in this village. He went on to explain that for many years, his vision gradually became worse. For a while, he could just hold a book a longer distance from his face and still see the words. But eventually, everything he tried to read became "blurry and too small."

His eyes were very dry. The extreme heat, dry sand, and relentless sun had taken its toll. As I considered what to say to him, I removed my reading glasses, which were perched on my head. Then it occurred to me. Maybe all he needed was reading glasses!

I asked him to try on my glasses and I turned to reach behind me for a book to use as a vision test. In those few brief seconds I suddenly heard, "One thing I do know. I was blind but now I see." He carried a small black Bible in his inside jacket pocket at all times. It was bookmarked to these words from John 9:25, which he was now excitedly reading with the assistance of these glasses.

His voice trembled with excitement as he explained that reading his Bible was his one daily joy that he treasured above all others. For years now, he had relied on his children and grandchildren to read his very worn Bible to him. But now, on this day, he was blessed to have regained his sight to read the very Word himself! This man was bursting with pure joy. And I was caught up in his excitement with joy for him. He looked up at me and through his tears said, "The Way, Truth, and Life are mine to read whenever I want."

Then he walked to the doorway, fully immersed in satisfying his hunger for reading the written Word. He did not seem to even remember that I was there. I smiled as I watched this man meander to his hut with his small black Bible in hand, and voicing page after page as if he was reading it for the very first time. I reflected, "If only more of our problems could be solved with a pair of glasses that clarifies our vision..."

I continued to clean the clinic and inventory supplies. About fifteen minutes later, I heard another knock at the door. Four more elderly gentlemen appeared in the doorway. The first to enter smiled broadly and said, "Doctor, we have come to have our cataracts cured." Each was grasping a well-worn small black Bible. I gave quiet thanks for being a person in need of having several pairs of reading glasses available at all times, for I always seemed to be misplacing them. I opened my backpack and found four more pairs.

I tried to explain that I was not a doctor, nor did I have any ability to cure cataracts or anything else. But the men just smiled. So I gave them each a pair of reading glasses and the story repeated itself, to the great joy of each of these men. I held up a small mirror so they could see themselves wearing their new glasses. Even James, who wore my very bright pink pair, thought he looked quite good in his new spectacles.

I surely did not cure anything for anyone on that day. But I learned that sometimes when you least expect it, you find that you have the tools to make a positive change even when you initially could not see that for yourself. My own eyes were opened wide that day. I saw how the Word can sustain a hungry community though many afflictions.

As night fell, I closed the clinic door. My eyes turned towards the village huts. I could see the men sitting in a circle, reading aloud. I gave thanks for the little things in life like reading glasses, and prayed that my eyes would continue to be opened to these new experiences.

Peace
(written by a boy, age 14)

Peace is the best gift that God has given to us.
It enables us to receive such good friends from all over the world.
Oh Peace, Oh Peace,
Know what a wonderful person you are.
May you live forever Peace, that is why Africa is blessed.
Oh Peace, Oh Peace,

If you had not been there, people were going to die,
People were going to suffer, yes, suffer, Oh Peace.
People stay in the villages because of you Peace.
People move at night because of you Peace.
People fly every morning and night coming to Africa,
    because of you Peace.
So God, thank you for what you have given us – "Peace"
People
Educated
And
Courage
Endless
Thank you God for Peace.

Iyan and Regan

Our team found little Iyan sitting alone in front of his hut in his village, just a little mass curled up in a ball of pain and high fever. His cheek was so stretched and swollen that he looked like he had a hard round ball pushing on it from inside his mouth. He had a large open wound on his upper neck. Upon further examination, we realized that this infection was actually coming from within his mouth and had broken through the skin below his jaw line.

I walked to nearby huts looking for some information on this boy, as he seemed to be all alone. A man who spoke some English told me the boy had been sick like that for a very long time. He had no idea where the boy's mother had gone. He thought the boy had a bad tooth and that someone tried scraping it out with a piece of glass. This was the result of a lingering tooth infection? A ray of sunshine beamed through the trees and rested on this sweet boy's angelic face. He seemed near death, yet he seemed to be just waiting for us to find him. Our team leader gently scooped him up and our team boarded our van to go in search of a physician. The young people on our team were suddenly very quiet and pale.

We found good-hearted physicians more than an hour's drive away to help with wound care and antibiotics. Throughout the journey, this little boy never cried, but his eyes pleaded for some comfort. X-rays later revealed that Iyan's jaw was likely partially eaten away by a tooth infection that had slowly progressed over the several months. While he was being treated, I tightly held one of our young team members as she sobbed uncontrollably for him, then I went to comfort two more of our young people who were struggling to comprehend how things like this happen in a world with so many resources to help. We talked about what a privilege it was for us to be here volunteering alongside these wonderful people.

Iyan's wound was treated, and our team leader handed him to me as he went back into the clinic to arrange for ongoing treatment. I talked to our young team members about how each of us might use our own resources and knowledge to help those in need and to raise broader awareness of situations like this.

Most of the team then left to explore the town. Iyan took some sips of an orange drink, then rested his head on my shoulder and sighed deeply. He fell asleep from sheer exhaustion. Everything else around me ceased to exist in that moment. My tears fell onto his warm face. I looked into the clear blue sky and whispered, "Please send one of Your angels to protect and heal this precious little one."

In this same village, we met Regan, a 14-month-old who had the head of a child his age, but the body of a mere six-month-old due to severe malnutrition. His mother was unable to nurse him, as she was quite ill and could not adequately care for herself. Regan had received only minute amounts of nutrition for several months. His six-year-old sister, Joanne, carried him all day long on her tiny back. Out of necessity, she had assumed the motherly role in his life. He was such a part of her back that she no longer seemed to notice that he was there. I wondered if she would ever be able to fully stand up straight again. I watched as she unsuccessfully tried to get him to suck on a piece of sugar cane.

Regan's eyes were listless. He was covered in sweat and dust. His pants were torn and soaking wet and they smelled terribly of body waste. My heart hurt so badly for this child. Flies landed on his face and he was too weak to shoo them away. His pain was so great that he never even bothered to cry any more. Is this what it means to be alive but dead at the same time? I slowly unfolded his tiny frame from his sister's back and gently cradled him in my arms. We helped him to sip some of my vitamin fortified water and slowly eat tiny amounts of peanut butter. In town I was able to purchase supplemented powdered formula – three large cans, covered in thick layers of dust, for thirty-five dollars each. Thirty-five dollars? I asked the store clerk if this was actually thirty-five US dollars. He assured me that was correct. That explained the layers of dust. The villagers make six dollars a month working in the fields. How could they ever afford this?

We taught his mother how to deliver the formula to Regan, and under the direct assistance and supervision of a caring neighbor who stepped up to help, his mother began to nourish him every three hours in this way. He began to show some improvement in his mental capabilities. His eyes appeared to become more focused, and he slowly but surely reacted when stimulated. At least that is what I wanted to believe as I watched him sip the liquid nourishment. As I kissed him goodbye at the end of this trip, I realized that the image of his little bones painfully pushing through his thin skin would stay with me always. And that is a good thing, for it helps me to remember that I need to share my own blessings more often and more abundantly with the Iyans and Regans of the world.

I went back to this same village a year later. There in the new school that this nonprofit had built over that past year sat Iyan, with a huge, happy grin on his face, looking so handsome in his school uniform. He was seated at the front of the class and while I could see the scar on his neck, he seemed to have fully recovered. When he saw us, and after getting a nod of approval from his teacher, he excitedly ran to give us all big hugs. His teacher smiled broadly. They then settled back into their classwork.

Later that day, when we were serving a lunch of chicken vegetable soup to all of the schoolchildren, Iyan, carrying his now empty bowl after happily consuming a hearty serving, approached me shyly and softly whispered something in a language which I did not comprehend. I looked to his teacher for interpretation. She listened to what he repeated, and explained that his words meant, "God is good." I cannot say for certain that is what he actually said, but his teacher was confident in her response. She grinned proudly and said, "I taught him so." As we sat in the grass reading the picture book we brought, no words could capture the contentment of that moment – this little boy pointing to each picture, and me, in total wonder of his healing.

I then went to find Regan. While he seemed to be a little developmentally delayed, he too was smiling and able to stand on his own little legs. He had gained some weight and loved playing with the ball that we brought for the schoolyard. But it was his big sister who sang his praises, saying, "My brother is good and fat." Joanne was standing much straighter, and she said with a broad smile, "Weebale, Amin." (Thank you, Amen).

Village children have taught me so much. Through them, I have witnessed light shine in the darkness. In your own volunteer journeys, you may encounter very sick children like Iyan and Regan. Treat them and their families with dignity and understanding. Do not judge their circumstances. Provide assistance within the limitations of your knowledge and capability to do so. Small acts of compassion can result in far-reaching effects long after you return home. Whether you ever know that or not really does not matter. What matters is that you tried to make a bad situation better and that you continue to learn.

Hunger
(written by a girl, age 12)

Hunger, Hunger,
You are a spirit that can make people do anything,
Good or bad things.
Hunger, Hunger,
Some people you kill,
Some people are imprisoned because of you hunger.
So what can we do to avoid you?

Fair Trade

Our volunteer team of fifteen members ventured into the city marketplace, which was packed full of men and women, each vying for our attention with the wares displayed for sale. In this place, selling was a vital key to survival. Tourists at times took advantage of this situation.

As I pondered the potential purchase of a beautifully hand-carved chess set, the board and animal pieces intricately detailed in ebony and teak woods, a safari tourist approached and offered the young craftsman a mere one US dollar for the set. This was well worth more than two hundred dollars if sold in a different setting, and the young man was asking for only twenty-five. With such stiff competition, he had made no money that day, and he had a family to feed. When I write that he had a family to feed, I do so with emphasis, for without a sale on any given day, his family would not have any food to eat on that day. Hunger was constantly lurking and the pressure to make a sale was intense.

The tourist opened his wallet, which was bulging with a great deal of cash. He brashly plucked a crisp new one dollar bill, which he began to wave before the crafter. The young man was visibly shaken. One dollar would buy a few pieces of bread for his children. But he knew that this chess set was worth much more. He knew the long hours he had spent carving, and he knew that asking for twenty-five dollars was more than fair. Seeing the young man's hesitation, the tourist haughtily laughed and tauntingly said, "If you really are so hungry, you'll take the money. Hey, I'll even add in two more dollars to make you feel better about it." For this tourist, it was merely a souvenir. To this young wood carver with a family to feed, it could be life or death.

So I stepped in and loudly and gingerly offered sixty dollars for the set, knowing that would infuriate this well-dressed tourist. And infuriated he was! His face turned red with rage. He turned toward me and roughly growled, "Just what do you think you are doing here, little lady? I am trying to make a deal with this peasant. And I had him down to three dollars!" Fortunately, the actual anger-laced words filling my head and on the tip of my tongue did not come out. Instead, to my own great surprise, I heard myself calmly and slowly say, "I am feeding the hungry and protecting the meek."

Now I assure you, these were not my words! Not at all. I was heading down a totally different path in my mind. And I was eager to explore that path as I felt him tower over me. Yet these alternate words were the ones that actually escaped my lips and they came out much more calmly than my high blood pressure reading and rapid heartbeat would have indicated at that moment.

The tourist paused and just stood there in silence. We all just stood there motionless for what seemed like an hour, but was likely actually less than thirty seconds. Finally he looked at me, the anger receding from his face, and he mouthed the words, "Thank you."

Then he opened his wallet once again and offered the young man $103 for the chess set and nicely asked to purchase several other carved items as well, all at a very fair market price. With delight, the wood carver packed his crafts with great care in old newspaper. I faded to the background as the two spoke, and I watched as they shook hands and smiled as the wrapped packages exchanged hands. And I gave thanks for the Voice within that spoke for justice for His people.

<u>What is Right?</u>
(written by a boy, age 12)

If you need help, I will fight,
Because that is right.
They came at night, took our parents in the night,
They took our sisters out of sight,
That is not right.
No one cared, we hoped that someone might,
That isn't right.
So if you need help, I will fight,
Someone must do what is right.

Photo Magic

In remote African villages, cameras are often an oddity. Children are always asking to see what they look like when a picture is taken. They love to just take your camera (and now, instead, your phone with the camera) and do photo shoots themselves. Most often, they take much better and more interesting photos than I do.

As one of our team members was performing magic tricks for the children at an elementary school, I took a picture of an adorable little boy who was observing from the sideline. He asked to see his picture. As he looked at himself on the display screen on the back of my camera, a very puzzled look came across his face. He touched his head, then looked at his picture in the camera. Then he touched his stomach, and did the same thing. Then he touched his arms, repeating the puzzled look back to the digital camera photo. Finally, he looked at me, and then pointed to the photo displayed on the camera, and said, "I know I am here," he said as he patted his head. "So how did I get in there?"

He had never seen a camera before, so seeing his entire image in the photo made him wonder how that could be – he was in two places at once! I smiled and explained how a camera works and that he was not actually inside the camera. He very seriously whispered, "I think it's magic." With that easy explanation, he ran off to play. Small volunteer experiences like this are so heartwarming and memorable. Maybe some of this just is magic!

Later that day, we traveled a few miles to the secondary school. I heard the older girls giggling as they tried to nominate someone to approach me. One girl stepped forward and asked me for a photograph. Her strong accent made it difficult for me to understand her request. She then made a square shape with her hands and motioned as if she were taking a picture. Finally I understood. So for the next few minutes, I snapped several pictures of each girl, then more shots of the girls as a group. They squealed with delight as they repeatedly viewed each photograph. The girl who initially approached me could not stop looking at her photo on the camera's LCD screen. She looked up with tears in her eyes and softly said, "I am pretty."

And indeed, she was a natural beauty. She continued on to say that she had never actually seen herself, only in the reflection of murky river water or a dirty cracked window pane. She had never seen a mirror. Imagine, never having seen yourself in all of the fifteen years of your life. Ever! She kissed my cheek and said, "Thanks Mum. I am happy." I am always so in wonder of how such simple little things like this bring such happiness.

Visitors
(written by a girl, age 11)

Far from Home,
Learning, expanding.
New things, always good.
New friends, always good.

Samuel

A teenager named Samuel looked very ill. He was so thin, so pale, and so weak. His stomach was very bloated. His mother said that he had experienced severe diarrhea for several weeks and had not been able to eat or drink. He needed to rest for long periods of time, as sudden fevers and chills frequently plagued him. He told me he had lost hope in living. I thought he was likely infected with parasites.

As we transported Samuel to the hospital clinic, he told me that he hoped to one day be a driver. I asked him why. He replied, "I will never own my own car. I will never drive my own car. So how fortunate would life be to then just drive a rich person in his car? And if I cannot be a driver, I want to be a pilot and fly people all over the world."

I felt the heat radiating from his body as we approached the clinic. He was drenched in sweat as he exited the vehicle. He slowly and shakily tried to stand upright with no support. I asked him to lean on me. He said, "Is it OK, Mama? With you being from the United States?" I assured him that it was way more than OK; it was my privilege to be spending this time with such an incredible young man. He managed a weak smile.

At the entrance to the clinic, I saw a small open window that was the point of patient registration. I led Samuel there to begin that process. As Samuel communicated his name and medical symptoms, he suddenly and visibly became tense and looked very sad. I stepped forward to ask what had happened. The clerk explained that Samuel did not have the exam fee. I explained that I would cover all costs on this day. She then charged me the full fee – which converted to eighty US cents. I thought that I had heard incorrectly. She explained that I must pay in full now in order for Samuel to be seen by a doctor. I assured her that the fee would not be a problem. Samuel solemnly promised to work to repay me. I greatly struggled with this. Eighty cents or he could not see a doctor, and he was deathly ill. And he thought that I had just paid an enormous sum of money. Even realizing the relativity of all of this, I remained so deeply saddened that sick people are not medically treated solely for the inability to produce less than one US dollar.

Once the fee was settled, we were given a blue paper booklet that would become his medical record. I was instructed that no one but the physician could write in this book, or the entire record would become invalid. Next we were directed to the creaky wooden door marked as the laboratory. Inside, the technician asked about Samuel's symptoms, which he again related in detail. They were speaking in a language that I did not fully comprehend, and I could not follow most of the conversation.

The technician motioned for Samuel to take a seat in the exam room to wait for the physician. She then motioned to me and repeatedly asked for what sounded like a matchbox. I was very confused by her request. I thought this must be a local medical term with which I was unfamiliar. I repeatedly stated that I did not understand. She pointed to the flame on her Bunsen burner, then made a motion resembling a flint striking the side of a matchbox. Finally I understood – she really did want me to provide a matchbox. But for what? And where did I find one?

She motioned toward some buildings down the narrow road outside of the clinic. So with blind trust, I ran down the dirt road and found three huts and seemingly no other person around. I stood in front of the hut entrances and shouted, "I need to buy matchboxes." That sounded silly, even to me.

Suddenly, a person appeared from each of the huts with matchboxes in hand. I bought five, spending the equivalent of ten cents. I raced back to the laboratory. The technician smiled at me for finally understanding what was needed. Yet I still had no idea what purpose these matchboxes fulfilled.

I watched as the technician dumped out the matches then cut each box in half. She handed two halves to the young man. He knew exactly what to do. The matchboxes were the specimen containers for his stool sample which the technician would test for parasites.

The technician prepared slides from the sample, and under the microscope easily identified that Samuel was infected with two different parasites. No wonder he had been so ill! She allowed me to look at the slides under the old but functioning microscope. I worked for several years in the United States as a trained microbiologist, so I appreciated this unique, hands-on learning experience.

The physician arrived and conducted an examination. He too reviewed the microscope slides and confirmed the diagnosis. He prescribed treatment and told me that I would need to go about two miles down the same road to find a roadside pharmacy. So off I ran again until I found a small white building with a weathered wooden sign marked "PHARMACY" crookedly dangling from a post above a window. I handed over the prescription, paid about four dollars, and soon had Samuels's treatment in hand.

Samuel had hope. And I still had so much to learn.

Stomach
(written by a girl, age 13)

Oh Stomach, Stomach!
Why do you make us work for you?
You cannot stay without water and food?
Why don't you work for yourself?
You make us move from long to short journeys
In order to get what you want.
Oh Stomach, Stomach!
Why are you so much work?

Underwear

Volunteers sometimes find themselves in situations where even the most basic needs of daily living are not being met. Sometimes focusing on one specific need can have a very significant impact, creating a positive ripple effect.

Just like women in more economically developed countries, women in rural Africa also have monthly cycles and are in need of feminine hygiene products. Why do I state the obvious? Because I have met many people who do not understand that women, wherever we live, have the same basic health care needs. And this subject of menstruation makes many people uncomfortable, as if to discuss it is taboo. Yet here it is, a critical monthly problem for so many women worldwide.

One of our new team members enthusiastically volunteered to coordinate a village project to introduce a wonderful reusable, durable feminine hygiene pad product. Made of soft flannel material and absorbent liners, this pad can be sewn for use with or without underwear (yes, many women have not even one pair of underwear). I had used similar pads supplied by an anti-poverty volunteer organization during my own young years growing up in a small coal-mining town, and had previously seen versions of this project successfully introduced to other impoverished areas of the world. So I was excited to see her launch the project in this village, and she did an amazing job.

This need was even more so brought to my attention during a school-wide celebration day in the village. As we prepared the luncheon for the event, a sudden wind sent our paper and plastic bags swirling across the sand. The little children jumped up and ran to retrieve the bags. Rather than returning the items to our table, they ran towards their homes with big smiles on their faces.

I asked an elder woman what was happening. She explained that often the young women cannot easily leave their homes for one week each month while they have their periods as they have no hygienic products. They use whatever they or their children can find – sometimes torn cloth, but more often mixtures of dirt and grass, newspaper, leaves, plastic bags, cow dung, or maize cobs. Then at the end of the week, they wash the paper and plastic to reuse them the next month. She explained that many women experience infections and great irritation from the newsprint ink and plastic. Can you imagine washing and reusing newspaper to stuff into your body every month, out of basic necessity?

In addition, I learned very few could afford the equivalent of two to three dollars per pack of ten store-purchased pads, and many stores did not even carry them. If the cost alone was not prohibitive, the disposal of these products was. Weekly garbage pickup and trash cans or bags for waste disposal were nonexistent.

I discussed this further with the schoolteachers. They concurred this was a serious problem for young girls in this village, and further noted that by the time a girl reaches adolescence, she is likely to drop out of school. Missing a week of school each month was just too emotionally difficult for her to handle, especially so when the lack of textbooks and writing materials necessitate the need for rote learning. And the anxiety of not knowing when day one will start each month caused some girls to just stop trying to make the long walks to schools. Many girls own just one school dress and if that is accidentally soiled, the girls are embarrassed and have no other proper clothes to wear. Several girls expressed the fear of being teased by boys when menstrual-related accidents happened.

With sewing patterns, material, thread, and needles in hand, our passionate and caring team member laid out the cloth, and prepared for our first class. Soon the women streamed in from their huts. After an introduction and education about the project, the women were ready to sew.

As I was assisting one of the women with threading her needle, I accidentally knocked over my backpack. A tampon fell from my bag onto the white sand. The irony of that situation left me wordlessly standing there, looking at it. I felt that it glowed like a neon light. Just then, a little girl scampered over, picked it up, and handed it to me saying, "Mama Denise, you dropped your pen." Children possess an uncanny way of making things OK!

As the sewing continued, a joyous chorus of women working alongside women filled the air. The excitement generated by this new product that would help make their lives a little less cumbersome felt electric. The female bonding was warm and wonderful as we embraced one another.

But I continued to struggle with the knowledge that all women do not all have the same resources and choices to meet our basic needs. And suddenly, and with self-disappointment, I realized I was part of introducing a product I had not yet tried myself in my adult years. The next day, I hired two village women to make two pads for me, and I used these pads myself for the remaining days of my menstrual cycle. And they worked perfectly.

At the end of this trip, we distributed underwear to all of the women who had participated in this project, explaining that these might make wearing the cloth pads a little easier. I held the large bowl filled with many colored panties, and offered the first pair to one of the older women in the group. She gleefully chose a bright yellow pair, then sometime later she asked, "Now, how many women do I share this with and how do I know who they are?" It took several seconds for me to understand that she might think that this pair of underwear was hers for one week each month to go along with the use of the pads, then rotated through other women before returning to her the following month. Was that what she was actually asking? I didn't know if I should ask for clarification or just respond.

So I replied, "This is for you, and only you." She looked rather stunned as she clasped her undergarment to her chest, and slowly said, "I am very, very thankful to be given such a new gift." Again, I had to take a few seconds to absorb what she said. I noticed her badly torn, ragged skirt and threadbare shirt as I began to comprehend that her reaction truly was sincere. Perhaps this was her first and only pair of underwear? Or maybe her first pair of new underwear, and in her correct size?

I was speechless for a few seconds more. No words could express the many mixed emotions that I was feeling. This was a pair of women's underwear, nothing more. But to her, in that moment in time, it was a special new gift. I enveloped her in a huge warm hug.

The remaining women were just as excited to choose their pair. The yellows and pinks quickly disappeared, followed by blue and white. Strangely to me, all of the purple ones were the last to be chosen. I asked why. The women replied that purple was a "royal" color, which they related to "rich." They did not feel worthy of that color. I assured them they were indeed quite rich in ways that many people never achieve, and indeed, that I myself had not yet achieved.

Our team members repeated this project in other African villages for the next decade. After completing this project in one such village and returning ten months later, I was approached by a young woman who had been waiting near our first-aid clinic. She asked to speak with me in private, behind the building. I followed her there as she led the way. I wondered what was on her mind as she slowly pulled up her long skirt. She wanted to discreetly show me that she was wearing one of these reusable pads. This woman had walked four miles to tell me how much this had changed her life. She was now able to leave her hut every day, any day of the month. She was able to cook and care for her children without the worry of dealing with her body's needs in more cumbersome ways. Like some of the women in the first project site, this woman had also formerly used a mixture of grass and mud, which caused great irritation to her skin. She smiled and said, "Now I am like you because I can be a moving woman all days." I liked that phrase: moving woman! We embraced, and I held on a little longer, grateful that she made this long journey to share her story with me.

In another village, we presented the pad project to the young girls who were still attending classes. The headmistress was thrilled, as she too noted the unsettling drop in female retention rates in school as adolescence approached. When we returned the following year, the headmistress excitedly described a 49 percent increase in female retention rate at the school. She felt that number would continue to grow to more than 75 percent, and she attributed this increase to the positive impact of the pad project. These young girls now had a realistic means to meet their maturing needs. The headmistress made several pads herself and stocked them in the first-aid kit in her office. She communicated to her students that if a need arose during school hours, the girls should come to her office and she would assist them. The retention rate continued to rise as these girls now had a practical and reliable means to deal with their changing bodies.

We also learned that some of the schoolteachers were now using these cloth pads. In doing so, they were absent from school themselves much less often, and they were even able to remain after school for some additional time with students in need of extra tutoring.

This project continued to grow and we added an extensive lesson about the anatomy of the female body, physical and emotional changes girls go through as they grow and mature, reproduction and childbirth, and any other related topics that the girls and their school headmistresses or elders felt that we should incorporate.

When we took this project to another African country, the high school girls were eager to learn. The headmistress shared that if these girls were unable to stay in school, their future would likely include early marriage to a much older man, and birthing their children at a very early age, as young as thirteen or fourteen years old. All dreams of becoming a teacher or nurse or accountant would be permanently dashed.

As we assembled for the start of the lesson, several of the high school boys entered the classroom. They asked for permission to stay for this project, and I noted immediate relief from the girls when I explained that this was for girls only. The boys walked away, but they looked quite sad. I wondered why.

During the class discussion about "being a girl and our changing bodies," we read one of my favorite books, *The Woman with the Elephant Heart*, in which our womanly thoughts and emotions that embrace our human connectedness are so adeptly captured. The girls related to the emotions expressed by the author through her words and incredible artwork. Their own elephant hearts did not miss a beat as they shared personal stories of their struggles of being young girls carrying heavy weights in life.

After the lesson was over and the pads were made, we exchanged friendship bracelets as a symbol of our bonding. It was then that I noticed that the boys had returned and were hovering near the door. One boy shyly came forward and asked if we had extra kits. As I tried to comprehend his need for that, he said, "For my sisters. They live far from here and cannot go to school because they have no supplies like this. I will learn how to make this and take it back to them."

Another moment of speechlessness struck me as I saw about ten boys eager to help their own sisters. That was the reason the boys had asked to stay earlier that day. As I handed out each kit, I was greeted with a broad smile and a sincere "Thank you, Teacher." No words escaped from me, as this deep love of family and enthusiasm for the potential opportunity for a girl's education overflowed in my own heart with love for these children.

Later that same day, one of the male teachers approached and asked if I had some patterns for him to take back to his home village, which was many miles north of our location. He explained that the girls there could not attend school due to lack of sanitary pads, and that they so longed for an education. He described the girls' painful experiences of digging a hole in the sand inside a dark hut, isolated from the main village site, where they sat for most of the five to seven days each month during menstruation. He stated that in that sand and soil lives what he called chiggers, explaining that it is like a small bug similar to a tiny spider that feeds on soft tissue. My body cringed at the thought of the plight of these young girls. We assembled several pad kits for him and he quickly and joyously ran off to deliver them.

The pad project lived on at this school long after this initial session. The girls who first learned to make the pads began to teach the younger girls as they matured and were now in need of these. The school's headmistress continued to invite girls to her small office, and often they were the ones who seemed most troubled by things they could not yet express. She served hot tea, and together they read sections of the elephant heart book. They discussed the many dimensions of being a girl, using the author's words and art to facilitate deep, meaningful discussion. She said, "After we read this book together, the girls are never the same – in a good way. This book touches their hearts and their positive self-esteem unlike any textbook we have ever used."

We had the privilege of taking this project to an African women's prison. Many women seemed to be there for reasons not quite clear to them. The head of the prison shared that some of the women were victims of violent domestic abuse. They longed for release, not only for themselves but even more so for their children. Our team was told that if a woman who was sent to this prison did not have someone to care for her young child, then she must take that child with her, and the child remains there until a guardian is willing to assume responsibility for the child, the woman's release, or until the child reaches the age of seventeen. (Since that time, the women's prison has worked very hard to successfully find foster families by the time a child is three years old.)

For those women who will be released within one or two years, having marketable skills to assure success is critical. Introducing the cloth pad project in this environment was a viable means to assist with successful reentry to life beyond confinement. The women enthusiastically welcomed this project, quickly learning to operate treadle sewing machines, and producing pads which they paired with bars of soap that we donated. This package could then be sold in the local villages. The money raised would in turn be used to buy food and medical care for the children who resided with them in the prison.

We learned that not only did these women continue making pads after our team's departure, they then shared this project in two other venues. One was at the adjacent "barracks" where the spouses of the men who are incarcerated in a different nearby men's prison stay with their children. These women have no means to support themselves and their children and they bear the stigma of their husbands' incarceration. So they moved to this very rudimentary community housing to survive. The prison's corrections officer was a wonderful, caring person, and she shared this pad project with these women living next to the women's prison. She told us that the availability and use of these pads was the number one reason that the young girls from the barracks were now able to attend school.

Furthermore, the corrections officer took six of the women inmates to a trade show. There they demonstrated to other women how to make these pads, and explained how their use can increase their daughters' retention rates in school as well as reduce infection rates caused by the use of rags and other unsanitary materials. The corrections officer felt this demonstration was high profile at the show and achieved positive success.

The corrections officer continued to embrace this project and expanded it even further. When a woman is released from this prison, she is given completed cloth pads kits to take back to her village and she is asked to take additional unsewn pads to teach the women in her village how to make these. The feedback from the corrections officer was that with this initiative, more and more girls in many villages are now able to remain in school. In addition, if a woman becomes proficient in sewing these pads on the sewing machines that our team refurbished at the prison, she could earn a formal certification in tailoring that could be applied to realistic employment opportunities upon her release.

What was initially a relatively small project has grown into a positive life-changer for these young girls and women. With a determined effort and a lot of listening to the local community in which you are volunteering, you can help to turn someone's adversity into something very meaningful. If the opportunity to volunteer at a prison arises, assuming any safety issues have been vetted, consider saying "Yes." If the prison residents offer their handmade goods for sale, and with the oversight and permission of the corrections officer, consider buying them at a fair market price. The women will likely use the money to buy food for their children.

A wonderful, energetic woman attended a discussion I presented back home in the United States about these pads and their direct tie to girls' education. I asked for a volunteer who can sew, and she beautifully rose to the challenge. Afterwards, she coordinated an ongoing effort to organize monthly sewing bees (social gatherings based around an activity, often for charitable purposes) to assemble and sew these pads. In time, and after her own trip to experience life in African villages, she started a nonprofit organization to sustain this growing and important project for girls in need in many parts of the world. Girls helping girls – how very wonderful indeed!

Over time, her sewing team grew and embraced the project as it continued to blossom. The shape of the pads as well as the fabric were modified and improved. Ties with embedded elastic that encircle the girls' waists were added to make it easier to hold the pad in place. The new bamboo material or fleece liners work quite well and are very absorbent. A waterproof liner made from recycled Tyvek envelopes was inserted in the pad. A cloth pouch for carrying clean pads and a waterproof pouch for dirty ones were welcome additions. This makes transport between home and school so much easier. A calendar to track cycles was added. Locally made soap is now often included as part of this packet. When feasible, washcloths are provided.

The initial educational component was expanded. A laminated written curriculum with text and pictures makes teaching the health and hygiene class easy for almost anyone to do. I reincorporated the use of a menstrual cycle tracking bracelet that grew out of the initial project. The girls greatly enjoy assembling the multicolored beads, which helps them to better understand the stages of their own personal monthly cycles. The bracelet-making is an excellent female bonding experience as well. On one trip, I asked my teammate to lead this part of the project. She sat on the rough cement floor of a partially constructed room, lovingly teaching the girls how to make these bracelets and encouraging them with her words. Our African project leader leaned towards me and said, "Christine is glowing. She has become part of the women here." And indeed, Christine's caring heart had melded into that circle of sisterhood.

Through the experiences gained while expanding this menstrual pad project, I learned that some teenage girls who have no access to feminine hygiene products were being sexually exploited, exchanging sex for a small pack of store-bought pads just so they could stay in school and not be forced to marry so young. With that came the risk of pregnancy and/or sexually transmitted diseases. These girls fully and enthusiastically embraced this cloth pad project, including the health and HIV/AIDS lesson that accompanied it.

While conducting the health classes with young girls who are orphaned, I learned that some girls were visiting the local pharmacy dispensary on a monthly basis to obtain malaria treatment medication. Without proper knowledge about puberty, these girls thought their monthly cycle of not feeling well and bodily bleeding was the result of malaria. The educational classes dispelled those misconceptions and minimized their perpetuation.

In several villages, daughters shared that their fathers refused to provide funds for menstrual pads so that they could attend school full time, with the belief that their daughters needed to be wedded as soon possible, and that schooling was a detriment to that. I make no judgment in stating that, for these families appeared to be doing their best to make ends meet. Their mothers did not have monetary funds, so they provided hems from their skirts or "knickers" (underwear rolled up inside of another pair of underwear) to use as clean menstrual cloths. We saw many girls enrolled in the early grades of one and two, but by grade seven, those numbers dropped drastically. We met older girls in certain areas who were selling half of their monthly food allowance just to buy pads. Many girls mistakenly feared that their monthly cramps were a symptom of stomach cancer. Health education, yoga stretches, breathing exercises, and cloth pads were welcomed in these circumstances.

Some of you reading this may still be feeling uncomfortable about this topic of menstruation. Yet it is a real-life issue for women. Until we are able to address these basic needs in some sustainable, affordable, realistic way, these young girls will feel the strong pull to drop out of school due to their fears related to their changing bodies. However, these girls desperately want to be educated. They do not want to marry so young. They do not want to be married to a stranger who is decades older than them. They do not want to be babies having babies. They will tell you so themselves.

When you volunteer with girls like these, take the time to hear the underlying roots of their struggles and how they press forward to overcome those challenges.

Education
(written by a girl, age 15)

Education is the best thing for our future,
Good education helps people find a better life.
If you are educated by people,
You can find happiness in your home.
Education is the best thing in life,
The fires all around you burn big and bright,
But the fire deep inside you will burn strong and light.
Education brings happiness, laughing – Be educated!
And smile when you have been educated by your parent,
For that is a precious gift.

Aesha

Our team's first-aid clinic was moving along briskly under the hot sun. One of the babies had a high fever, a runny nose, a slight cough, and no other visible medical symptoms. Her mother stated the local folk healer had recently chanted over the child in an effort to drive the fever from her body, but that approach had failed. Even after our team's treatment with over-the-counter medicine and cool water baths, the baby's fever continued to rise. We watched as she grew more listless. Her mother pleaded for a cure. She asked me if her daughter would die.

I prayed, "Help me to see what I am missing." Malaria. It just popped into my head. Aesha did not have all of the classic symptoms, but that word reverberated in my head. I needed to get her to a hospital for appropriate diagnosis and treatment.

The baby's fever continued to worsen, as did her breathing. Our team's driver had been away for most of the day, busy purchasing supplies. When he returned, my teammate and I transported the baby, her mother, an interpreter, and three other sick children to the nearest local hospital, a fifty-minute drive. I sat in the back of the vehicle in an extremely narrow crawl space meant for a small spare tire. One side of my head touched the back of the hot plastic seat, while the other side of my head pressed against the hot glass of the back windshield. The heat and dust made it difficult to breathe back there and I fought feelings of claustrophobia. But all I had to do was look at the faces of these sick little ones, and I knew that my discomfort was nothing in comparison.

We reached the hospital and raced the baby inside. After we paid a fee, she was immediately admitted for examination. With rapid testing, a malaria diagnosis was confirmed. The physician said this child likely would have died within another day without treatment. The good news – the physician agreed to admit her to the hospital. Then the bad news – the hospital was out of all medications that she would need. We sent a courier to the nearest city for assistance, which would arrive a few long hours later. Meanwhile, an intravenous saline drip was started as the nurses tried to keep her hydrated.

The ceiling fans in the hospital ward were not working. Thick dust coated the blades. No breeze flowed through the room. The room temperature was oppressively hot. The nurse explained that no funds existed for electricity to run the fans. Women and children filled every bed. And no one spoke. All of those people in one room, and yet the silence was deafening.

My teammate headed back to our project site while I remained to await the delivery of the medicine. I stepped outside to clear my head and to regain my composure. I watched a small monkey stride across the branches of a tree as he gingerly swooped near me at times. I stood in the inviting shade of the tree, and I wondered what I would do if this monkey landed on my head.

My rambling thoughts were interrupted by a gentle tap on my shoulder. A man apologized for interrupting and asked if I was the person who had brought his daughter to the clinic. After confirming that to be true, he asked if he could trouble me please for some food. I said I would be happy to do so, what did he need?

His eyes flew wide open and he emphatically said, "No, Mama, it is not for me. I will be fine. But we have no food. When someone goes into the hospital, the hospital cannot provide food either. So the family must bring something for the one who is sick to eat and drink while they are here inside the building getting medical treatments." That concept had never even occurred to me.

After assuring him that I would take care of the food and water for his child, I went back into the long rectangular ward with the beds practically on top of each other. I counted eighteen patients, each with a different diagnosis, including dehydration, malaria, tuberculosis, diarrhea, diabetes, and asthma. And although it was later in the day, it was still so stinking hot in that room. The white wire bed frames were topped with plastic mattresses covered with thin ill-fitting cloth. Some of the patients were sweating profusely, their skin sticking so uncomfortably to the mattresses.

I asked the hospital administrator how we could help. She explained that only four patients had food and water at this time. She also confirmed that the hospital ran out of funds to pay the electric bill so the ceiling fans were shut off a long time ago. The facility had little income and did its best to serve those who were very ill. Clearly the staff here worked diligently and were committed to providing as much quality health care as their means allowed.

My teammate returned from our project site and I explained the situation. We drove into town and purchased supplies for all eighteen patients, and some extra food for future patients. We paid the electric bill, including funds to cover future months, and had the power restored. We bought white cotton material for makeshift sheets. Our total bill was less than $100.

As I watched the nurses distribute the water, and the patients eagerly take measured sips, such great sadness overwhelmed me at not knowing how else to help in a way that would be sustainable. The girl's father reappeared and said, "My child will be well. The doctor tells me so. Her brother died from malaria but she will live. She is meant for something important. I, her father, will assure that she achieves that."

He was smiling. Not just smiling, but grinning from ear to ear. I offered him some food. He ate half, then tucked the other half into the torn pocket of his shirt. "For my wife," he said. "She never eats."

Just then that tree monkey dropped to the ground. We could see how thin this animal truly was. The man removed the small food pouch from his pocket and threw a piece of it to the monkey. The monkey gingerly picked it up and ran back to the tree. We watched him take small bites, as if he was thoroughly enjoying his surprise treat.

The man laughed as he watched the monkey. I must have looked quite puzzled at sharing his small amount of remaining food with the monkey, for the man matter of factly explained, "All God's creations here hunger and must be fed."

Food
(*written by a boy, age 11*)

Food, you are needed by everyone,
You make us happy.
Without you Food, our stomachs shrink and contract.
You are our savior from our enemy, Hunger.
Without you, there is no life.
Food, you are Life.

Soup(er) Man

Children at the village primary school had a new, popular friend, a genuine, warm-hearted man who had been part of our volunteer traveling team many times. On most school days, the young students received a very thin weak porridge. Our team member decided to change that to something more nutritious, and he began to cook delicious soup concoctions – with real vegetables, rich broth, and "wiggles" (the children's name for the broad wavy noodles that he brought with him to add to the soup). This was cooked outdoors in a huge pot of water over an open fire fueled by wood. You might imagine what a big, smoky, and laborious undertaking that is when cooking for more than one hundred people. Soon after our team member made his first batch of wiggle soup, our team was riding through the local town in our transport van. Children recognized us and ran alongside the van for as long as their legs could endure. When they recognized our chef, they cheered, chanting "Soup Man! Soup Man!" We all smiled at that!

On a different trip, I watched the children slowly lick the soup off of the noodles, then dip them back in the broth again and repeat that. They seemed to be trying to prolong this dining experience for as long as possible. Soup Man's cooking soothed many ailments on those days.

As soup was being prepared in a different village, the effects of hunger, one of the significant hardships that many villagers endure, made itself known in a way that I had not anticipated. Soup Man made a big batch of vegetable soup, and this time he added chicken. The children lined up for a bowl of soup and then ran to the back of a nearby building to consume their meal. After what seemed like such a short amount of time to eat a big serving of very hot soup, I saw them run from behind the building to refill their empty bowls. Then I watched that happen for a second time. I walked behind the building and saw small piles of vegetables from the soup lined up on the dirt ground. I watched as the children returned from trip number three, and noticed that they drank the soup, devoured the chicken, but added to their vegetable piles.

I gently asked why they were doing this. One girl explained that they do not ever eat something as delicious and special as chicken, so they were drinking the soup, eating the meat, and making the pile of the vegetables, so that they could then more quickly get another serving of chicken to eat. They had been told that they could return for additional helpings as soon as their bowls were empty. They fully intended on eating their little piles of vegetables; they were just trying to maximize the prize chicken and hoping that the supply did not quickly dwindle.

The girl continued, saying the chicken tasted so good and someone had told the village children that it would fill their stomachs and make them stronger with muscles because of something called protins (protein). And they wanted to feel not hungry; they wanted to feel stronger. Sorrow for these children filled my soul. They simply were hungry and knew this was not a meal they would see again for a long time. I again questioned how children in any part of this world could be so hungry when the world is bursting with food, much of which is discarded daily. But for today, our kind Soup Man was not only filling these tummies, he was filling their entire little beings with his abundant goodness. I pictured him with a T-shirt emblazoned with the capital letter "S" for "Souperman."

I realized why I was often so wrong when I tried to guess the ages of children in these villages. They seem so small and so much younger than their actual years, but they just did not have enough sustenance, enough protins, to grow. I fervently wished we could make starving children a thing of the past.

In many African villages, three meals a day is a foreign concept. I strongly urge volunteers not to eat their packed lunch or snacks in front of the children. If you do need to eat during the day when you are working in a remote village that has minimal food resources, consider doing so with respectful discretion, perhaps in your team van that is parked away from the bustle of the village. If you share with one child, many more children will appear in seconds, looking for their share. Planning for this will make meeting your needs and their needs go much more smoothly and with less disruption.

Hunger Hunger Hunger
(written by a girl, age 14)

Hunger is a great enemy which disturbs the intestines,
Every day people cry because of hunger and minus food.
Hunger will demand, and it demands that you look for food for it to stop disturbing you.
Children cry because of hunger,
Endless crying because of hunger.

It is such a great enemy, who brought it into this earth?
People have to grow so many crops,
  but it is never enough to fight this enemy.
It has led to the death of many people, just because there is no food.
Death is around us, so we need to take care.
Oh Hunger, you are a great enemy.
You have made many people suffer because of you.
You don't mind if the person is big or small,
No, you demand for everyone to feel hunger!
Oh Hunger, I wish there was a way
  that I could chase you from this country,
Maybe then people could survive,
  because we have lost most of them to you.
And we miss them because of you Oh, Hunger.
What can we do because of you?
Oh Hunger, you are truly our great enemy.

HEAR ME ROAR!

I found music classes to be an effective way to draw out young people's thoughts. Equipped with a Bluetooth speaker and an iPhone loaded with carefully chosen songs, I headed into the village classroom.

I explained that Bluetooth technology allows electronic devices to connect wirelessly, and that we would need to pair these two devices in order to hear the music. I turned over my phone and my portable Bluetooth speaker to four of the students to allow them time to determine how to make that happen. It took them several attempts, but soon we had paired devices.

Next I handed out the lyrics to the songs that we would be studying, as well as pictures of each of the artists with a short biography attached. Samplings of pop, rock, country, folk, soul, jazz, classical, movie themes, spiritual, and blues were included.

We started with the first song on the playlist, and the students eagerly followed the lyrics, then loudly sang along the second time. Every time we sang, the room filled more and more robustly with their beautiful voices. Several students stood up to dance and the comfort level in the room was high.

For each song, we discussed the musicians and their life stories, as we slowly read the song lyrics again. The students then tried to determine why that person sang that song. They were totally engaged in discussing artists such B.B. King, Bob Dylan, Pete Seeger, Michael W. Smith, Katy Perry, Pharrell Williams, and others. I marveled at how quickly they were able to associate song lyrics with events in that artist's life. They keenly understood the depth of pain and sorrow or joy expressed in these songs, and often from where that emotion derived. They asked about B.B. King's guitar, Lucille. They wanted to know more about what life in the world was like when Bob Dylan wrote "Blowin' in the Wind." And they wanted to know if I had a Justin Bieber song too!

In the end, they all voted for their favorite, which to my great surprise was Johnny Cash's "Ring of Fire." We played that song at least six times, as they wanted to memorize the words. Katy Perry's "Roar" was a close second though. When that song was played, they stood up and did hand motions for biting their tongues, holding their breath, and brushing off the dust. And they stood up even straighter during the chorus and roared so loudly that they could be heard at the other end of the school. I very much enjoyed watching them express themselves through this music. These students had the eye of the tiger and they were fighters for survival.

They sang these songs over and over again for more than two hours. The sound was glorious and I never tired of watching them follow the words as they more deeply grasped the intent of the songs with each recitation. We talked about the troubles that some of these musicians have experienced in their lives, and how they used their music to work through some of that.

At the end of the class, one girl who seemed to be rather shy and reserved stood up to speak. Everyone became quiet. She said that she too has difficult times in her life, so difficult that she cannot yet talk about them. But she said, "I will work now on writing a song about it all to express my fears and my hurts and my pain and find peace in my heart. I will write it tonight and sing it for my mother tomorrow. I can forgive after that happens." With a quiver in my voice, I encouraged her to do that, as I handed her my notebook and pen for her writings.

The other children ran off to their next class, and I could hear them loudly singing "Ring of Fire" as they descended the school stairwell. But this girl stayed for just a little longer, and with tears in her eyes, simply said, "Thank you, Teacher. May God bless you and your family."

Like poetry, music is a powerful educational tool. Bring your favorite songs with you and share them with the children in the villages and in their school. They especially enjoy hearing you sing. They will sing for you in return. These are beautiful relationship building moments.

Talent
(written by a girl, age 14)

Talent is any gift given to man by God,
People are unique with their talents.
One day at school, I will never forget,
Cause we saw a girl, unique to the rest.
This girl can make her legs be up and her head be down
    and dances very well, like no one else.
She told us good things,
That patience pays off,
That no one is perfect,
That no one is an island.
That makes me happy in a million ways,
And one day I will be like her.
So I try to be my level best,
And if you try, you can join us too.

On Eagle's Wings

The Circle of Sharing had already begun when I joined in. Eighteen African women were sitting on the ground with their hands folded on their laps and their knees bent to the right. Their long colorful skirts were tucked into the sides of their legs to keep the wind from ruffling their clothing. I listened as they talked about things like their children, the wells that were in working order and the ones that were not, the government food rations that might be available in the town center about a two-hour walk from their homes, family members who were ill, a woman who had given birth to a baby boy earlier that morning, and crafts that they might consider making together to earn money to buy food.

I listened intently, wanting to take in all that these strong women had to teach. Talk turned to more serious issues, such as sparse food supplies due to the long spell of extreme high temperatures and no rain, and late school fees with no immediate way to pay for their children's education. Three of their children were suffering from malaria. One woman said that her husband is now HIV positive. The women exchanged supportive nods of the head with each other and a few comforting words. One of the women turned and asked me if I had anything to say.

I responded with a sincere appreciation for the gift of sharing this space with such incredible women. I asked, "How do you deal with all of these adversities which never seem to end?"

The oldest of the circle smiled and said, "Child, close your eyes and hear this song." I obediently closed my eyes. They began to sing a tune that I had heard many times in my travels and in my own church.

> "And He will raise you up on eagle's wings,
> Bear you on the breath of dawn,
> Make you to shine like the sun,
> and hold you in the palm of His hand."

The woman, speaking in a soft, soothing voice, continued, "Keep your eyes closed. Now picture Him holding you in the palm of His hand. Picture Him holding you gently, protecting you from all harm. Let yourself feel the peace of that image. Remember this feeling of peace. Burn it fast into your mind and your heart. Hold it there. Now open your eyes."

I opened my eyes and looked out at the entire circle intently looking back at me. They were all smiling. Another woman said, "That is how we do it. We allow ourselves to be held in that Peace." All of the women nodded in agreement.

Before now, I had always thought of this song as one that is associated with funerals. Today I heard these words in a new way, as the embodiment of peace. I am a worrier by nature. On the most difficult days, I continue to close my eyes and picture myself being held in His palm. In that moment, all worry dissipates as it is replaced with the hope of being raised up on eagle's wings. In my volunteering, I am a frequent learner. Wherever you travel, listen at least twice as much as you speak. Some would say that is why humans have two ears and one mouth.

Mother
(written by a boy, age 13)

Mother, Mother, Mother
Mother is my gold in this world
She cares for me always,
She advises me when I have gone worrying.
Mother, Mother, Mother,
She looks like my earthly God because she makes me happy,
And she is very friendly too.
She makes sure I go to school, every day.
And she makes sure I have something to eat, every day.
She makes me feel like a president at home,
Because she gives me such good care.
Mother, I will never forget you.

Water Wonders

As the work on the village's solar well installation continued, the remainder of our team prepared peanut butter and jelly sandwiches for the schoolchildren. It was a very hot day and the sky was cloudless and robin's egg blue. The village women toiled near the well as their husbands worked tirelessly alongside our team members to convert the old manual hand-pump well to a solar powered pump. The solar panel was installed and the men were working to connect the water supply. Cattle and goats, with their rib bones clearly protruding from their bodies from lack of adequate food sources, sauntered lazily nearby.

I carried handfuls of biscuits and cups of juice to the men working on the well. It was early afternoon, and this was their only food of the day. One of the elder men saw me watching the others eat only one of their three biscuits, and then carefully place the rest in their pants pockets. Some of those pockets were more hole than pocket, so the men tied the shredded material into a makeshift pouch. The elder man whispered, "That is dinner for their children for later." I struggled with the disparity of that, and the knowledge that I would not go to bed hungry later this same night.

The village school is perched on a small hill, with the well work easily visible below. A few of our team members, including me, and the school's teachers stood on the hill under the welcoming shade of a tree, distributing sandwiches and juice to the last class of very hungry and appreciative school-aged children. A slight breeze ruffled through the leaves on the tree. Just then, the quiet was broken by the joyous sound of adults and children loudly rejoicing.

I turned my head toward the sound and looked down toward the well. I witnessed the most incredible sight. The men were testing the new solar pump, and abundant water burst forth from a hose that they had attached to the well. The men gloriously celebrated their great success with cheers and handshakes. Just then, one of our team members held his thumb partially over the end of the hose, spraying the children with an arc of water, as they shrieked with joy and wonder. This spray of water, in the brilliant illumination of the sun, created a magnificent rainbow. The children repeatedly put their hands in the free flowing water and drank from the hose nozzle with glee. At the appearance of the rainbow, the village women humbly dropped to their knees, their hands stretched upward to the sky in abundant thanksgiving for this precious gift of water. No longer would they spend twenty minutes or more laboriously pumping just five gallons of water. Now, it gushed from the hose, and their yellow plastic containers were quickly filled.

I stood in awe of this perfect moment in time – simultaneously, a rainbow arching over the children as they laughed and played in the spray of water, the men in camaraderie celebrating the success of their hard work, the women kneeling in reverent prayer of thanksgiving, my hands covered in sticky peanut butter and jelly. Even the cattle lifted their heads to look! What an incredible gift – the vision of such joy being celebrated in these different ways but with hearts united in that rejoicing and in the glory of that vivid symbol of hope and new beginnings. Suddenly, nothing else existed other than this scene playing out below me. My eyes filled with joyful tears. The emotional perfection of that moment is forever etched in my mind.

A schoolteacher stood beside me on the hill, taking in this same view. She reached for my hand, and quietly said, "Look! We are not forgotten." That is one of those moments when a warm squeeze of the hand is all that is needed. No pot of gold at the end of the rainbow expected. Just the comforting knowledge that one day the troubles of today would pass and peace will take its place.

She grasped my hand and said, "We go!" And go we did, down the small hill to wash our sticky hands in this wonderful water blessing and to join in the rejoicing.

I am just an average person with no special talents. I am not a risk taker. I am actually an introvert. The series of events that led me to this volunteer work continues to surprise me. But one thing that I can say for certain is this: Keep your heart open; keep your mind open. Serve with a humble posture. And when you least expect it, a door to heightened awareness and new insight about life's mysteries opens. Sometimes it is heralded by an unexpected sign like a rainbow. When that door opens, walk through it with eager anticipation.

Enemity
(written by a girl, age 13)

Enemity does not discriminate,
It is as common as trade.
It does not mind of the age,
All of us are taken at higher grades.

But it creates hatred.
Enemity does nothing to help us,
However much we hate people, we shall not gain.
So stay away from Enemity.

Wisdom: Out of the Mouths of Babes

The fourth grade students excitedly observed as I handed out the white cotton T-shirts and bottles of puffy paint. I asked them to use the paint to draw something important to them and in the colors in which they saw that. They carefully painted yellow and orange suns, red and purple flowers, pictures of our team, their village huts, their families, the well where they pump water, birds in the sky, their school building, soccer balls, a church, and a few things that I could not quite recognize.

As we waited for the paint to dry on the shirts, I gathered several of the students so that we could talk. I asked, "Tell me something that you have learned that you feel is very wise."

One girl spoke up immediately, and said, "If you are filled with pride, then you will have no room for wisdom." She shared that her grandfather had taught this to her mother, who taught it to her. She did not know her grandfather, as he had died before she was born, but her mother said he was a very wise man.

Another girl said her grandmother tells her, "When things are so bad, let go. God will catch you or provide you with wings to fly. But He will not just drop you on your head on the ground."

One of the boys stood up and proclaimed, "My father, he says: If you can solve your problems only with a fight then you must find another place to live." I asked him if he ever tried to solve a problem with a fight. He said, "No, I like where I am to live with my family. And I am a good talker. People just want me to stop talking so they move away and there is no fight."

One of the girls stood up and said, "What's inside the package is known only to its owner. My father told me this. He told me that when I get older I will understand. But I think I know. I think it is about when people look at me, they think they know me. But only I know me. The same thing is true of you and you and you. So we should not judge people before we know them. And even then, we may not know the sorrows they carry in their bodies." This little girl looked solemnly around the classroom, then sat down with great satisfaction in sharing this wisdom with her friends.

For the next few minutes, we sat in silence. The silence was calming, not uncomfortable. Then a girl who had been very quietly listening suddenly said, "Frog." I waited, but she said no more. So I asked, "Frog? That is what you learned that is wise?" "Yes," she said with no emotion, "Frog." Again I waited. Still nothing more came from her other than a bashful smile. I concluded that her frog and my conception of a frog must be two different things. Perhaps it was a word used in local tribal language. I made a note to further research that.

Just then, the children were called to get in line for the distribution of chicken soup, which our team had prepared. As I watched them run outside, I realized how much wisdom they already have at such a young age.

After lunch, I gathered the young T-shirt artists for a group picture. They eagerly donned their now dry artwork and happily compared each other's pictures. They walked off to play, happy with their artistic expressions. I sat on the ground and closed my eyes, soaking in the sunshine and my blessing of spending this time with these children. I felt a tap on my head, and heard a quiet voice say, "Frog." I opened my eyes, and the little girl was standing before me with a broad smile and the gift of a large handful of grass. She bent down and whispered in my ear, "My clothes, it means Fully Rely On God." Then she ran off to be with her friends, with her dark green blob of paint shining on the front of her T-shirt. I absorbed that for a few minutes before it hit me – FROG!! THAT was what she had abstractly painted on her shirt? FROG is something that I had taught to my own son many years ago, but had completely forgotten until now.

What fun she had with me that day! And what delight I took in this lesson from such a little one. Be patient with the little ones. As they grow to trust you, they will always come back to be sure that you understood the message that they were trying to convey.

Poetry

(written by a boy, age 11)

If I met a crow, I should say caa-caa!
If I met a lamb, I should say baa-baa!
If I met a cow, I should say moo-moo!
If I met a dove, I should say coo-coo!
If I met a dog, I should say bow-wow!
If I met a cat, I should say meoooow!
If I met a crocodile, what should I say?
I should just say, RUN AWAY!

My Ears Are Ringing

My eighteenth trip to Africa was on the horizon. Excitement was mounting as we neared our team's mid-January departure date. For some team members, this would be their first experience in rural Africa. Others were ready to return to an amazing medical clinic and see the newly opened adjacent maternity center.

About four weeks prior to our departure date, I developed tinnitus, a constant ringing sound in my ears. It appeared suddenly, and I initially thought that I could learn to easily adapt to my new normal. However, since other more severe symptoms accompanied this change, I sought an evaluation by a clinician. My symptoms appeared to coincide with the physician's more serious diagnosis, and I was prescribed a high dose prescription medication. Unfortunately, this medication not only exacerbated the tinnitus, it amplified the sound in my ears to the point where I incessantly heard the equivalent of a loud train whistle. It also came with other less than desirable side effects. I mourned that I lost what had been so precious to me – the sound of silence. Many tests followed, and ultimately this initial more serious diagnosis proved to be incorrect.

As I weaned off of the medication, and dealt with the permanent tinnitus, I acknowledged that I might not be well enough to make this trip to Africa. But my dear kind friend Theresa, who I tease about having unicorn magic, kept me in her prayers, as did my devoted husband. When our departure date arrived, I was well enough to travel, although I was still adapting to the relentless tinnitus. But I had my waterfall noise machine to help mitigate the silence of the night so that I could try to sleep, and I had the determination to adjust to this new change. And I had my two prayer warriors cheering me on.

It is not unusual to have celebrations with our African friends during the evening hours after a long work day. Often music blares from a speaker, and joyous laughter fills the air. Dancing to the music is a natural progression. I was still learning the sounds that trigger significant and unpleasant amplification of the ringing sound in my ears. I quickly experienced that this very loud music was a trigger that I needed to avoid.

One day, as my unicorn friend was hosting a celebration with the local children, the noise and music triggered very unpleasant amplified tinnitus. So instead of joining in the celebration, I carried a plastic chair to the grassy hill overlooking this event. It was high enough so that I could observe the fun, and far enough away that my tinnitus could slowly readjust to a lower level of intensity.

As I sat there watching Theresa happily blow bubbles and the children leap in joy and laughter as they tried to catch them, I noticed two village women sitting behind me on a blanket. They were waiting for relatives who were being treated at the medical clinic. I do not know how long they had been there, but I sensed that they had been observing me for some time.

Suddenly, I felt two different hands resting on each of my shoulders. Both hands had a caressing gentle touch. As I looked up and saw the women who had been sitting on the blanket, they smiled, but with an expression of concern for me. The woman in the bright green dress asked me why I was not down below celebrating with my American friends.

I explained my condition, then simultaneously, both women said, "Yesssss. We felt that from you." The woman in the orange dress said, "Now we pray for you. Close both eyes, Mama." And for the next five minutes, with their eyes closed and their hands on my head and shoulders, they prayed that God would deliver me from pain and bless me with improved health and comfort in my distress. They sang in unison about their belief in the healing power of God and asked that God help them to lift me up in prayer.

I felt a sense of peace wash over me. In that moment, I knew that I would find a way to adapt to this change in my life. The weakness and sadness that I had been feeling about not being able to join in some team activities were washed away and replaced with a feeling of thankfulness for these two women, neither of them previously known to me, who blessed me with kindness and concern.

As the prayer ended, we embraced, me with tears of joy, they with smiles gained from personal experiences of hardships and how they are overcome. The woman in the green dress said, "You have a purpose that only you can fulfill. Go to the wooden shelter and allow that purpose to be known to you."

With that, they gathered their blanket and departed. I sat there for a long time, reflecting on what they shared, and for the first time in a month, feeling faith instead of fear. And it felt good.

Later that day, I went to the wooden shelter, which was actually a gazebo built to honor a wonderful physician who was instrumental in constructing the medical clinic at which we were volunteering. It was early evening and as I sat on one of the railings near the high brush, I suddenly noticed that I could not detect the tinnitus. It took me a few minutes to realize that the sound of the chirping crickets in the shrubbery negated the ringing in my ears. I laughed at the revelation, then gave thanks for those two wonderful women who guided me to this place.

While I continue to always have this ringing in my ears, I was able to adjust my expectations and work on holistic healing. And at night when I sleep, the channel on my noise machine is now set to the sound of chirping crickets. So finally, I began to achieve the good deep rest that I had been lacking for so many weeks.

The night of the bubble party, our team met in the gazebo to exchange experiences from our day. We passed a talking stick from person to person, and the sharing of each personal story was so moving. When my turn came, I planned to pass. But as the stick was handed off to me, I heard this whispered in my head: "Tell your story."

So I shared my story of these two amazing women. I talked about how small acts of kindness, of taking the time to care for someone in need, can help correct the course of lives for people who are trying to gain or regain a foothold. These women were instrumental in getting me back on the path that I was meant to follow. When I close my eyes and concentrate on that day, I can feel their gentle touch and hear their song of healing. If you as a volunteer are ever approached by women like these, welcome them into your space. They will fill it with grace and peace.

Cream-Colored Butterflies and Hope

I watched the luggage carousel go round and round and round, thinking somehow that if I just kept watching, our team's remaining fifteen bags of project supplies would appear. I thought about the twenty-eight-hour journey behind us, my aching back, my lack of sleep, and the very busy weeks ahead. I wondered if all of this planning and work and time away from my dear family actually meant anything in the big picture of life. I knew I was overly tired and a bit of a crabby-babby. And then this beautiful butterfly, with cream-colored wings outlined in black velvet, fluttered over the luggage carousel. I watched its beauty and grace in flight and found my tiredness dissipate as my heart filled with loving anticipation of soon seeing our African family. This symbol of renewal and hope danced as the bags continued to revolve, and I was reminded that what was in those missing bags was far less important than what we were carrying in our hearts.

I pushed my luggage cart out into the dark night where our African friends awaited with smiles and hugs. All was good with the world again. But ten steps later we walked through a massive wall of black flies. Never had I seen such an enormous amount of bugs! They flew into my hair and my nose and even my mouth. Ugh! Many large bats flew overhead, easily getting their fill of this flood of flying dinner with each swooping pass. But soon we were greeted by the rest of our African family, and the broad smiles and tight loving hugs enveloped us once more. Our wonderful driver gave me a smile and a big hug and said, "Hope has returned." As I offered my own warm greeting, my energy began to refuel, and I was ready to begin another African journey.

Over the next two weeks, we saw firsthand how the projects initiated by our American team in collaboration with our African team were flourishing. Many had already become self-sustaining. Children were in school instead of laboring in the fields. Women had income-generating projects. Gardens produced food. And love abounded all around.

A few days after our arrival, we journeyed to the local women's prison, where we were blessed to have permission to conduct volunteer work. As we met with the women and shared some food and basic supplies that we were approved to bring, another cream-colored butterfly with black velvet markings outlining its wings floated overhead. I smiled, for at that very moment, our African project manager was asking the women about what they need. I heard replies of toothpaste, toothbrushes, soap. He asked them in earnest, "What do you really need?" The replies then were "peace" and "hope." He smiled in agreement.

Days later, as we traveled by bus to the village for one last visit prior to heading to the airport, I reflected on the privilege I have been given to share time and experiences with these wonderful people of Africa. I looked out the window at the children running as fast as their thin little legs would carry them alongside our bus. And just then, that same species of a cream-colored butterfly flew by my window. I arrived at this trip a caterpillar, but the inherent beauty of Africa once again unfailingly transformed me into a butterfly.

I thought about the word "hope" and how we all need that in our lives. Hope for these children, hope for their mamas and grandmamas. Hope for the orphans. Hope for the women in prison. It is the hope that volunteers and donors all over the world give when they support legitimate sustainable projects that work to help those in need, and do so respectfully. The African women often say, "Thank you for loving us." And that, I think, is what hope is all about.

<u>Success</u>
(written by a boy, age 13)

Success is what we all long for,
It's what we all dream for,
It's what we all hope for.
But success is not for all of us,
Success belongs to those who seek it.
Success is for those who yearn for it.
Success is for those who work hard, tirelessly for it.
For in the end, success is not a given,
	but what we must always work for.

Dancing in the Light of the Lord

Church in parts of Africa is often an all-day event every Sunday. It goes on for several morning hours, with a break to care for the children, then back for evening prayer. Everyone does this with willing devotion and joy. My first mass was a delightful celebration of song and dance. Everyone sings and dances. No one cares what your voice sounds like. The sound is beautiful to all for it is the gift you were given. And you are expected to use it!

On my first trip to Africa, our team attended different Sunday worship services held in the villages where we were volunteering to learn more about this part of village life, as several faiths peacefully coexisted within the community. Each was a joyous day full of celebration, prayer, reflection, self-discovery, singing, and dancing. Peace and love filled the air as the church erupted into drumming and dancing when the strains of this heartfelt song were lifted up in prayer:

> We are dancing, we are dancing,
> 	we are dancing in the light of the Lord.
> We are happy, we are happy,
> 	we are happy in the light of the Lord.
> We are happy, we are dancing,
> 	we are happy dancing in the light of the Lord.

And they were happy dancing in the light of the Lord. Many people ask me about African songs, as I often bring home videos in which people are singing. Singing is deeply ingrained in this culture. Children learn to lead group singing at early ages, and they eagerly do so with no prodding. Many non-African people who I have encountered seem to have a perception that Africans sing primarily as a way to deal with their suffering. More often I have seen that they sing because they have such faith and hope in God, and their singing is actually an expression of that.

These songs frequently reflect what is most important in the culture of the village. Quite often that is faith, family, and friends, in that order. I have witnessed how this kind of deep, open, committed passion and love of God and life expressed in song can contribute to healing and peace of mind for the people who reside in these villages.

I engaged the village school's headmaster in a discussion about the singing. He is a faith-filled man who said one of his greatest joys is being surrounded by the schoolchildren under a big tree in the schoolyard, with them singing a song called "We love you Jesus." He had been at this school for thirteen years, although he could have been making much more money working in a city school. He walked twelve miles every day, from his house to the school and back. His clothes were dusty and his shoes and socks had big holes in them from wear and tear. Yet he clearly was a happy man. I asked him why he remained at this remote school for so many years. He replied, "If I leave, no one will be sent to oversee this school and the children's education. I cannot be at peace if that happens. These children deserve to be cared for." He told me he searches every day to discover what God has put inside of him to make a difference in the world.

I asked him his secret to happiness. He said, "Whenever I feel that God is far away, I feel sad and lonely and uncertain. So I ask myself one question, 'Who took the first step?' For always, it is not God who took the step away. And all I need to do is simply step forward again to start feeling better in my head and heart." One step forward. That is very good advice. During your time in Africa as a volunteer, you will likely meet many people like this headmaster. Dedicate time to get to know these people who are full of wisdom borne from life experiences.

I looked around this village one last time before beginning my journey home. Images of brotherly love danced before me as I watched the boys interact with each other and their friends. I saw one of our team members playing peek-a-boo with two little girls. Every time that he "peeked" around the corner of the school building, the girls laughed uncontrollably in delight. Another team member was leading the children in a rendition of "head, shoulders, knees, and toes." Children were swinging high on a wooden swing that our team carved and hung from a high tree branch. I saw young mothers nursing their newborns as they lovingly cradled them in their arms. I saw village men whittling tree limbs into works of art.

As I gazed at the beautiful children running to school, I heard a song in the background which sounded so familiar to me. The voices of the young men sitting on the side of the school building grew stronger and resonated throughout the schoolyard. With harmonious voices they sang:

> I, the Lord of sea and sky,
> I have heard my people cry.
> All who dwell in dark and sin,
> My hand will save.
> I, who made the stars of night,
> I will make their darkness bright.
> Who will bear my light to them?
> Whom shall I send?
> Here I am, Lord. Is it I, Lord?
> I have heard you calling in the night.
> I will go, Lord, if you lead me.
> I will hold your people in my heart.

"Here I Am, Lord." A song that I too had sung in my own church. I turned to give them my full attention and appreciation of their beautiful harmonies. I asked, "Why are you singing this song?" The oldest of the group was in his early twenties. He explained that a Roman Catholic priest regularly visited the village at least twice a month over a five-year period until he died of a sudden illness. He was a very spiritual man who had guided these boys though their most difficult youthful years. He had cried with them when their parents died of HIV/AIDS. He taught them how to be heads of households even though they were just barely teenagers themselves. He taught them about the love and forgiveness of Jesus. And this was the song he sang as he worked in the village. They often heard him singing the chorus as he approached their village in the early morning hours.

I learned that this priest walked long distances to serve this community. He brought with him material needs like scissors for the midwives and taught them how to properly clean them in preparation for an infant's birth. When he was able, he brought them whatever food he could find. He spent much time just listening to anyone who needed to be heard, encouraging those in need of hope, and comforting those in deep sorrow. His homilies were discussed for days after the worship celebration had ended. This priest had greatly earned the love and respect of these young people. His passing was a time of great mourning for this village.

Then, suddenly understanding this song choice was not a random choice, I asked, "Why are you singing this song for me?" The eldest again replied, "Because we know you are leaving us today. We hope you return soon and also bring people who God is calling to come here to help us." He paused, then continued, "And when you go back to your home in the United States of America, we want you to tell your people that God's children live here too."

Tears clouded my vision as I looked upon God's children before me. Prior to this first journey to Africa, I had been struggling with my own self-confidence to be able to do this ministry. This song was the answer to my prayer for direction. And when I returned home, I carried their message with me as I held His people in my heart. And I am a witness that God's children surely do abide in these rural African villages – dancing in the light of the Lord.

In 2014, I attended a concert by the composer of this song, Daniel Schutte. As I told him this story about the blessings that his words carry afar, his eyes glistened with happy tears. What an honor it was to be able to share this uplifting story with the man whose words were so far-reaching.

Many times, I have walked behind a building in Africa or retreated to my room and privately wept for those who could not or would not weep for themselves. Every time, those same people taught me how to turn those tears into dancing. When you are in an African village, come prepared to sing. On or off key is just fine. And come prepared to dance. Graceful or clumsy is just fine too.

"THAT"

There are days when I say, "Things cannot get worse." Yet they do seem to get worse. There are days when I say, "Things will get better." Yet they do not seem to get better. I struggle at times with the concept of "hope"; however, Africa is teaching me the meaning of hope.

When I have the privilege of being part of life in an African village, I make time to just sit under a shade tree, away from the hustle and bustle of the day's activities, and watch what unfolds. I see children who are babies themselves so lovingly caring for their younger siblings. They do this with true love of family and respect for their parents, with no sign of this being a burden. I see mothers walking for miles with the great weight of a full jerry container of water perched on their heads, babies swaddled on their backs, and laughing and sharing stories with each other. I see them reprimand their children for bad behavior, then look at the other mothers with a nod and an understanding smile that seems to say, "We take great pride in raising our children with manners and respect." I see love expressed as a bonded community. I see people who I know are very ill raise their faces to the sky and smile broadly as they take in the warmth of the sun. I see people of all ages who are struggling with great adversity go about their day with no complaints. I see children laughing with glee as they play with cars made of mud and sticks, or soccer balls made of crumpled old newspaper. I see people truly rejoice in the glory of a new day unfolding.

And so very often I watch people wake up in great pain, or not knowing how they will feed their family on that day, or how they will tell their children they can no longer attend school as they cannot afford the school fees. Sorrowful funeral processions for children under the age of five are common. At times, the long walk to fetch water ends with finding a broken well instead, and no water in sight. You see people whose sclerae, the whites of their eyes, are yellow due to malaria. You see young pregnant mothers who are suffering from severe anemia due to malaria. You see some of those mothers deliver very low-birth-weight babies who sometimes do not live for more than a few days. You see children with distended stomachs that look like they are ready to burst due to intestinal worms. You hear that the medications that can easily treat these types of infections are often unaffordable or unavailable. You see children who are so deathly ill from eating from "dust bins" (garbage containers) or from drinking from sewer pipes. Any emotional joy you felt is replaced with emotional turbulence.

And in these moments, I see something which I call "THAT."

"THAT" is what these villagers have. It is what I desire. I want to have the confidence and courage to wake up in the morning, and for my main focus to be so very grateful for that one day. I want to believe deep in my heart and know in my head that today is a gift, a perfect gift that I have been granted, a gift to cherish and use to the best of my ability, no matter what lies before me. Each day I have 86,400 seconds to be an instrument, to live, to love, to forgive, to smile, to praise.

Every single day should be lived like that and embraced. I want to open my eyes each day and face the good and the bad, be filled with joy for a new day, and with the strength and conviction to never waste the precious gift of each and every day. I want to solidly know that my faith is always strong enough to carry me through any day, through any trial, no matter what, without question. I want to stop whining and complaining. I want to embrace acceptance of whatever the day has in store, while always closely holding onto faith and hope. I want my scars to be symbols of strength. I want to be able to truly forgive any and all hurts. I want to challenge myself to ask that with all of the craziness in this world, with all of its disappointments and calamities, what is my role in making things better? I want to celebrate my present moment of being alive and to be appreciative for everything, just like I see lived out in Africa. I want to respect the journey rather than working toward some end goal in life. I want to dance, to sing, to rejoice in my faith, and more so in times of struggle. I want to choose joy.

In these villages, I witnessed what deep, unwavering faith is, what power it has to heal hurts, to wrap itself around you when you need comfort, to brighten what can become very dark places in our hearts and minds. I learned that peace is not found in material things, but it is found in faith and trust in our Lord. I have always known this, but until I achieved this level of understanding of what "THAT" means, I could not understand how these people, in all of their poverty, hunger, and pain, could be happy. Yet, they were happy. Very happy. I recognize and understand that this concept is one for which some may disagree with me; however, this concept revealed itself many times in my travels.

On every trip, I find that for all that I take to Africa, I bring back home so much more in my own head and my heart and soul. I learn from the strength and resilience of the African people. In their poverty and in the face of the brutality of wars or survival in refugee camps, they feel blessed to be given a day, each day. In illness, they find new strength and unity. Without solicitation, they tell you how blessed that they are. It is humbling to be in the midst of such people and their love of life, which they consider to be the greatest of all gifts.

The spirituality that I witness in African villages is at a level which one day I hope to attain too. There in those villages, my heart swells with the goodness of those people, my eyes become more open to the real struggles of people who are just like me but born in a different place, and my mind becomes open to new realizations and truths. In Africa, every person tends to the needs of the other, regardless of material resources. In Africa, community matters a great deal.

I asked one lovely woman how she is able to share so much when she herself has so little. She replied, "We each do God's work in helping anyone who needs help. There is always something to share." I asked her how she knows what to do in these situations. She smiled a knowing smile and advised, "Just be still and listen to the Voice." I am still learning to be still… and to listen.

I have so many blessings here in the United States. But I don't have "THAT"– that unblemished joy that fills the villagers when they open their eyes each and every morning. And while I am still far from "THAT," my hope is that with each moment that I spend with the enlightened and wise people who live in these African villages, I am taking steps to grow mentally and spiritually stronger and continually move a bit closer to "THAT."

People look at my pictures and often say, "Oh, those poor people! They have nothing." I say, "Look again. For in the midst of seemingly nothing, they have everything." Truly, I have never met happier hearts or more peaceful minds.

Dignity
(written by a boy, age 15)

If you want to have dignity, you need to take action.
Making a man requires more than just saying I am sorry,
It means learning to change.
Apology is just the beginning.
The most important thing is to display honesty,
    courage, and compassion when you extend your apology.
You need to learn forgiveness too.
Love and life are important, but everyone makes mistakes.
And what we learn is to let anger go, and keep love young forever.
Success and happiness can be attained by those who have their dignity,
So you should respect yourself and equally respect others.

PART II

Harsh Realities: Finding Hope in the Midst of Suffering

As your volunteer experience in Africa expands, you begin to see things beyond a one-dimensional lens. You see the joy, but you also begin to see the more difficult aspects of volunteering, experiences that challenge you physically and emotionally. You may encounter people who are deeply hurting, but who hold on to hope with conviction. You may find yourself surrounded by scrawny street children earnestly begging for money or food. You may see levels of poverty you never knew existed. Your path may cross hunger and thirst that threaten the very existence of life. You may experience cracks in your own team's unity and cohesiveness. You may have days when you question if the work you are doing is causing more harm than good.

As with the joys of volunteering, the harsh realities are personal learning and growth experiences. Your understanding that wherever you go, people are truly the same, will become even more clear through these harsh realities. These experiences are not emotional highs, but neither are they just emotional lows. They are a means for volunteers to personally witness the delicate balance of life, that fine line between life and death that many people walk as each new day unfolds, and the amazing strength and resilience that embody those people.

As a volunteer, you will learn there is an equilibrium between the joy and the sorrow that needs to be found deep within yourself in order for you to be effective in your purpose for being in Africa. You will learn the difference between sympathy and empathy, and how to use those emotions most appropriately. At times you may find yourself not knowing how to respond or how to act or react. Through those experiences, you will need to find your own inner reconciliation to what you can and cannot commit. When you achieve that balance, that is the moment when you begin to feel the strong steady beat of a passionate volunteer's heart.

Zaira

Children love to sing for visitors. Is anything more joyous than the sound of children singing? Children in these villages endure many significant hardships. Education remains the key to providing a less harsh struggle for them. Village schools embrace that and are doing the best they can with what resources they have to teach these children. One of the songs often sung, and emphatically so, by the schoolchildren is "We LOVE education. We cannot be a nurse or a teacher or a driver without education. We want to learn. We want education. We LOVE education."

Spirituality flows abundantly in these villages. One of my favorite animated songs performed and sung at one of the village schools is "Let us be singing, let us be jumping, let us be dancing in the name of God. Just let it be, whatever it will be, just let it be." The children joyously jump and dance and swirl in the moment of just being alive.

On a return visit to Africa, my teammate and I planned to visit a village school located near our worksite. We traveled to the school with great excitement that day, knowing the students had planned a welcoming ceremony. Freshly painted white rocks lined the entrance to the school as a special greeting for us. The classrooms were built in 1954 and the structures were literally falling apart, piece by piece. The grey bare walls were embedded with huge fissures. At times, large chunks of rotting wood from the roofing fell onto the children. The windows were missing or broken, allowing the thick outdoor dust to settle on the children or the heavy rains to drench the classroom.

Students sat on the cement floor, which was a very uncomfortable bed of many deep jagged cracks. When the sparse blackboard chalk and paper supplies were depleted, the children were moved to the school's outdoor courtyard, where they sat on small rocks in large semicircles under the searing heat of the sun. They completed their lessons in the sand, using a twig in lieu of paper and pencil. The children's only food for the day was served in the evening, and consisted of a small serving of rice or mealie meal (corn meal porridge). The children often struggled to fully concentrate on their lessons, especially when the weather was so very hot.

Yet these children were eager to attend school, and they loved to learn. Never does one hear a single complaint from these little ones. They have great respect and love for their headmistress and their teachers, who were incredibly dedicated to these students. The teachers must live at the school due to the remote location, and their tiny and sparse living quarters were also in need of great repair.

Fifty-nine orphans attended this particular village school. Twenty-nine were at significant risk of death over the next few years. They were growing up with few of their basic daily living needs being met. Their caretakers, most often an elderly relative with very few resources and often who was battling personal health issues, could not adequately support the physical needs of a young child.

One of the students, who was an orphan herself, told me she would like to be called Zaira. She pulled a thin, worn piece of paper from her skirt pocket and recited this poem for us:

Life As an Orphan

The day my parents died it was my last day to smile.
It was not my fault to be orphan.
When the rains came, they treat me like a street kid.
    Rags are my clothes.
I do not have special clothes to wear on the weekend.
    No one likes to buy clothes for me. I am alone.
My life is in danger. When the rainy season starts,
    I went to the fields to work.
When I came back home early, they beat me
    and told me to go back to the fields.

When they eat rice, they give me only sadza.
Sometimes I wish to live in a children's home.
  Playing with other orphans.
  What is it like to just play like a child?
  What is it like to smile again?
There is no one to love you.
It is very hard to live without your parents.
The End

I struggled with my emotions as she read this with such defiance in her voice and fire in her dark brown eyes. She was just a thin little girl, standing before me in torn, ragged clothes, with no smile, with such a heavy weight on her shoulders. I hugged her and asked if she would do me the honor of helping me make peanut butter sandwiches for everyone. A very slight smile crossed her face. Then she looked up and very seriously asked, "What is this peanut butter that you speak of?" I grasped her hand as we ran off to explore the answer to her question.

We served the schoolchildren and the local community peanut butter sandwiches and juice. This was met with great enthusiasm, as tasting peanut butter was a new experience for everyone. Also, this was one of the very rare times that they would ever eat during the middle of the day. Three children asked me why the peanut butter sticks to the roofs of their mouths. Two seemed certain that their tongues would never become unglued to the peanut butter. Four asked why it is served on two large slices of bread as one meal instead of two or four smaller servings. Several asked what the "brown soft paste" was. Several others asked how a "brown bean" (their term for peanuts) turns into soft paste.

I watched them seek shelter from the hot sun under a big tree as they munched on their sandwiches. Having walked three miles to school with no food to provide nourishment, the children were slowly and deliberately relishing each bite. They grinned as they held the peanut butter in their mouths while it slowly melted. They good naturedly teased each other when some of the peanut butter landed on someone's nose or cheek. And they were joyously laughing and singing. I loved watching them just be carefree children for this short time.

Next we handed out school supplies. The pencils were distributed first. As I reached for the notebooks, I heard, "snap, snap, snap." I had forgotten to explain to the first class that we had brought enough pencils for each child to have his or her own pencil. In these villages, a new pencil is a great possession. Without being told, a child who receives this gift will instantly snap it into two or three equal parts to share with other children. That was the snapping noise that I had heard.

"Stop!" I shouted. "Don't break your pencils." One little girl with big, brown eyes and long, curled lashes looked up at me in wonder. She held up half of a pencil and said, "I keep this one?" I told her she could keep both halves. With a puzzled look she asked, "For certain? Both?" I replied, "Yes, for certain." She asked if there would be enough for everyone then. I assured her there would be. She smiled and, looking at the pencils in her hand, happily said, "Yes, for certain then. TWO pencils to keep myself at the same time. Today is very, very good, Mum."

The children spontaneously broke out in song. The chorus included these words: "I want to thank you, Lord, thank you, Lord, from the bottom of my heart." Once again, I had to fight back my own tears. This was a pencil that we were talking about. One whole unbroken pencil per child. And they were thrilled and thankful.

As the light of day faded, we prepared to leave. Each girl had received a new dress as part of our supply distribution. Zaira, wearing her new dress, hugged me tightly and I did not think I could ever let go of her. When we parted, she handed me a small square that she had saved from her peanut butter sandwich. She said, "For your journey." I could not find a big enough hug to thank her, as I wrapped her tightly in my arms one last time. She smiled, ever so slightly, as she told me that the water from my eyes was making her dress wet. Little did she know that the water I was holding back would have been enough to soak each and every one of these precious children.

One little boy tapped me on my shoulder and asked if we were ever coming back. Before I could reply he pointed at the freshly painted white rocks lining the school entrance and said, "We made that so you can always find us." I told him not to worry; we would definitely find them again.

Grace

Twenty-two-year-old Grace arrived at our team's medical clinic holding her three-week-old daughter, Precious. This beautiful little baby had been born with one of her hands missing most of the finger bones, resulting in small projections of skin and soft tissue where the fingers would have developed. Grace feared this was a very bad omen.

Precious was quite healthy and we assured Grace her daughter would very likely learn to function with the use of her two hands. She also told us about her energetic two-year-old son, and her smile was engaging as she beamed with great pride about her children.

I sat with Grace as her son played in the schoolyard. After getting to know each other better, I asked Grace this question: "Of the many things that you must deal with each day – walking for miles to get water, the lack of adequate food supplies, the droughts, malaria, HIV/AIDS, scouring for firewood, caring for your children – what is the single most difficult thing that you have to deal with every day?"

Without hesitation, Grace replied, "Hoping that I make the right choice for my family. I am both mother and wife. Many times we have only a very small amount of food to eat to keep our bodies alive. Every day I think to myself, 'Grace, do you eat a little bit of that food and hope that it will help you to live long enough to see help arrive in time to save your family? Or do you accept that help will not come soon to this country, and that then it is better to give all of the food to my children?' For if I do that, although I will not be here longer to care for them, they may live longer for help to reach them."

Never could I have predicted that very direct and realistic response. Her most difficult decision each day is to eat or not to eat. To live longer to care for her children and hope that assistance will come soon, or allow them to live longer in the hopes that help will eventually come to them. I looked at her again. She was so thin, so frail, with eyes so full of love for her children. The choice she was making was clear.

Her words resonated deeply with my own experience of being a mother. What a tremendously difficult decision to face each day, knowing that either choice greatly affects your young children and their futures.

We dressed baby Precious in a new bunting and blanket, and provided Grace with some food and other basic supplies. We embraced, and then she walked home, turning to wave and beam one last captivating smile. I watched as she and her children laughed and played along the path.

Grace's words made me reflect on difficult decisions I have had to make, none of which were such definitive life-and-death decisions for my family. I worried about what would become of them. I wondered what choice I would make if I were in her shoes.

Helen

Our team arrived at a secondary school to interview the ninety orphans who attended class there. We hoped to expand our child sponsorship program, and needed individualized information about the children who attended this village school. We had a standardized list of questions to ask each of them, including age, gender, form (school grade or class) attained, likes and dislikes, personal needs, what they wanted to be when they grow up, and with whom they lived. The children sat under a big, leafy shade tree, waiting for their turn to be interviewed. All were chewing on tree bark at one point or another.

As we interviewed these young teens, we heard many sad stories. Some children now lived with an aunt or uncle or grandparent. Often the scenario involved up to nine people living in one small hut, in very crowded conditions. Food was extremely scarce. Some children walked eight miles to and from school each day. These children greatly missed their parents.

One girl was twenty years old and still in high school. Her mother had died several years earlier due to complications of HIV/AIDS. Her father, who was also HIV positive and quite ill himself, was so distraught that he threw himself into the path of an oncoming car. She explained that while her uncle provided her with a place to sleep, he could not provide funds for her school exam fees of thirty dollars per semester or assist her with any other basic living needs. So she worked in the nearest city one year to raise money for her educational fees, and then attended class for the following year until she depleted her funds. Alternating these tasks extended her graduation date, but she was fiercely determined to become a teacher. I asked her why she chose teaching as her future career. She replied, "Our only chance of survival here is through education. We must learn all we can and use it to make our country a better home for our children and their children. I will educate our children."

The next girl also expressed a desire to become a teacher. Her goal was "to encourage our youth to never give up on their dreams." She said she would teach her pupils to speak good English so they could find jobs.

Another girl excitedly talked about wanting to become a nurse. She explained that she often experienced headaches and did not feel well when she walked the daily six-mile trek each way to school and back. She sought care at a neighboring clinic, but very sadly stated, "No one there listens to me. They just give me a pink pill and say take it and you will be fine. I am not fine when I take it. I feel worse. And they don't hear me when I say that. So when I get older, I will be a nurse and I will listen to everyone who stands in front of me and is sick. And I will make them feel better."

One boy dreamed of being a driver. With a twinkle in his eye, he explained he knew that he would never earn enough money to buy a car. He reached into his pocket and produced a worn, rumpled paper. He slowly and carefully unrolled this to reveal a picture of a shiny red sports car. He said, "This is what I will drive for people. Or maybe even a big truck. I will never have a car for myself, but I will be very happy driving other people's cars for them. And I will be very safe on the road and watch out for animals." This dream not only made him very happy, but provided the motivation for him to stay in school.

The boy's best friend stepped up next. He said that he did not want to be a driver like his friend. He wanted to be a patriot. I asked him what that meant. He said he wanted to be part of his country's military because he loved his country and wanted to work to make it a safe and happy place for his people to live. His respectful ask was for a pair of shoes. He said that it is hard to be a patriot if your feet are not wearing shoes. He made a very good point.

A very fragile-looking boy sat down beside me next. He continuously munched on his tree bark as we talked. He said his mother was very ill and he was the head of his house since his father left. His thin shoulders were carrying a heavy load. His sunken eyes looked so tired. He said he liked going to school and enjoyed learning. His favorite subject was math. He added that he disliked hearing his younger sister cry. I asked why she cried. He replied, "Because she hungers. So I give her whatever little I have to make her stop the crying."

Many of the parents of these children died during childbirth or when the children were less than three years of age. According to the teachers, HIV/AIDS-related illnesses were responsible for the majority of the deaths, although the children most often stated they did not know how their parents died, or they attributed it to malaria or tuberculosis.

Just then, Helen sat before me as my next student to interview. At fifteen years old, she was surly and impatient. Both of her parents had passed away from HIV/AIDS. She was raising her younger brother and sister while caring for their elderly grandmother. I asked her the standard question, "What do you need?" The most common responses we had been hearing were clothes, school fees, food, paper, pencils, pens, shoes, a satchel, soap, an exercise book for school, and moisturizing lotion. Not one child asked for anything outside of his or her own immediate needs for survival and education.

Helen simply and crisply said, "Food." In an effort to elicit more of a response from her, I asked again, "What else do you need?" She again replied, "Food." Once more, I asked, "So other than food, what else do you need? Maybe shoes or pencils or clothes?"

At that point, she quite firmly set her pen on the table before me and emphatically replied, "Only FOOD. For with food, I could think. And if I could think, I could do anything."

What amazing insight she had at only fifteen years old. Her response clearly explained the significant downward trend in the students' progress reports that I had reviewed earlier that morning. For without nourishment, without food, they could not think, they could not focus. They could not adequately learn and retain their lessons.

The cause and effect of the hunger that these young people experienced began to materialize. The clues were there in the interviews. I was just not intently assimilating them until now. These children rose before dawn to gather water from the well and to tend to other chores. Breakfast was often described as "green tea" (boiled grass and tree leaves) for girls, nothing for the boys. Then the long walk to school in the hot sun with no water and no shoes followed. The first and only meal of the day was provided after school at six in the evening. It was usually a cup (and literally just one cup) of mealie meal (porridge) and occasionally "okra" (tall thin grass-like greens from the fields). For some, the food supply was so minimal that dinner was served only on alternating days.

As I continued to review the teachers' written assessments of these students, the trend now jumped from the pages. In the elementary school years, when the children received a small school-sponsored lunch each day, the teachers' student assessment journals documented descriptions of the children such as "very bright; eager to learn; great potential; good math skills; does well in writing; good attendance; good student." Then, as these children aged and progressed to the secondary school, where no food was available, the entries began to reflect "trouble concentrating; cannot seem to focus; has the ability but does not seem to be able to retain learning; falls asleep in class; not studying; attendance issues; not working up to ability."

After this three-hour interview session, I looked up at the sixty orphans before me. Their clothes hung on their thin, bony frames. They were still chewing on the tree bark. Earlier that day, I reasoned this was akin to mindless chewing on a toothpick. Suddenly, I recognized that they were chewing on the tree bark to combat their hunger pangs, not as a "cool teen thing" to do, as I had originally surmised. The long walk to school, no breakfast or lunch, a cup of food for dinner was all made more real to me now. Their inability to focus was clearly linked to the lack of food in their stomachs. As Helen said, "…for with food, I can think…." Without food, their minds could not maintain focus.

As the interviews concluded, we served a lunch of fresh bread, peanut butter and juice for everyone at the school. When we returned to clean the dining area, I at first thought that someone had already done that. The tables and plates were immaculately clean. I saw the last two remaining children wet their fingers and touch them to the few crumbs of bread on each of their plates. Every morsel of food was consumed. Not one crumb remained.

We returned the next day with rice, cooking oil, vegetables, bananas, bread, beans, and other staples for each child to take home. Later, we prepared land for planting an orchard and delivered seeds for the school garden. It was food to nourish their bodies and minds. For with that very basic need met, they could begin to think. And for those with the spirit of Helen, they then could do anything.

Together As One the Child Should Live
(written by a girl, age 14)

Together as one, the child should live.
Physically and mentally,
Ready to achieve,
Together as one, the child should live.
Overworked and over strained,
Over stressed and underfed,
Sick and dozing in class is the result of that.
Early in the morning the child shivers like a chick.
Physically and mentally, not living as one.

Esther

While coordinating a basic first-aid clinic in a rural African village school, I became acquainted with a lovely teenager named Esther. Esther had been suffering from headaches and her teacher sent her to see me for evaluation.

We talked for several minutes and I learned that Esther rarely drank any water. She explained she traveled on foot for an hour to reach school each day, and on her return trip home, she had to carry a large container of water back to her hut. She did not drink any of that water as every drop was needed for cooking and washing. She had a loss of skin tone, parched lips, a rapid heartbeat, and frequent muscle cramps. Her mother had died from complications of HIV/AIDS.

Esther and I talked about how our bodies need and use water, especially in this very hot climate. She was fascinated to learn that our bodies are about 50-65 percent water. Esther confided her fear that her symptoms were related to HIV. We sent her for diagnostic laboratory testing to be sure and she tested negative. She was relieved and elated, and so was I.

I asked Esther her age and she replied, "Sixteen – more than half of my years of life are gone." In her village, the life expectancy of women was only thirty-two years of age. When phrased like that, from the mouth of a teenager, the thought of being middle aged at sixteen was both stark and stunning to me. Truths like these are always so difficult to absorb.

In turn, Esther looked deeply into my eyes, and asked "So, what is your age, Mum?" I smiled and told her that I was old indeed. She mischievously replied, "I share my age, now you must share yours."

I smiled into that shining face and replied, "Forty-eight." She gasped audibly and then slowly raised her hand to gently rest it on my shoulder. Then, looking directly into my eyes, and with the most reverent voice that I have ever heard, and with such great sincerity, she said, "Oooooohhhhhh! You are sooooo old!!!"

And I realized that I truly was, having already lived more than fifteen years beyond her own life expectancy. The rest of the week, Esther followed me wherever physical work was to be done. She carried water and supplies for me, and anything else that I needed. She took such good care of this little old lady. I asked her what she wanted to become when she grew up. She smiled and said, "But I am grown up! I do want to be a mother, and I want to grow old, at least forty years in total."

"At least forty years in total." That was a dream for the girls in this village. Meeting Esther made me realize that to achieve her dream, her basic needs would be food, clean water, and occasional access to health care. When I look around this world of ours, with all of the food, water, and medical capabilities, I wonder, why do people need to die at the age of thirty-two due to starvation or contaminated water or treatable illnesses? I was determined to learn more about what I, as a volunteer, could do to help make this dream come true.

<u>Death</u>
(written by a boy, age 14)

Death,
Death, Death
I fear Death, One day
Death took my Dad, I started to cry,
that is why I fear death. People came to the burial
for my father, I remain alone, even now. Death is hopeless
That is why people fear to die, They want to just eat when people die.
But once it will come to you. And more will feel alone and fearing it too.

Third Grade

As we approached a village that I had visited a year prior, I began to see signs of the significant effects of the ongoing drought conditions. The land was parched and the crops were shriveled. Wells were broken and people were walking several extra miles to find water. Cows and goats were moving much closer to where people lived, desperately searching for food themselves. A local man shared that elephants were circling remote villages at night, looking for farm fields to raid.

The food rations that we carried for the villagers were much smaller than in past visits due to lack of local goods to purchase. When we visited the nearest town's grocery store that morning, only a few items were left on the shelves: beer, condoms, and exercise books. No food. The drought and failing economy had indeed taken a great toll on all aspects of life here.

Our team received permission to interview the orphans in the primary school. We knew the number of orphans in this village was rising, so we wanted to better understand the specific needs of this population of children. My teammate and I entered a combined classroom for third and fourth grade students, about seventy children crowded around about 15 small wooden desks. The children immediately stood up, straight and tall, and in loud unison said, "Hello, visitors. You are most welcome here." Then they sang joyously and emphatically for us and in appreciation for our presence at their school. This was my team member's first trip to Africa and he was immediately enthralled by these children. We wiped tears from our eyes as their faces beamed with pride and their harmonious voices filled the air.

As the children took their seats, we introduced ourselves. Then the teacher asked all orphans in grades three and four to stand. On my previous visit to this same classroom one year earlier, about 25 percent of this class rose in response to this request. This time 75 percent of the class rose from their seats. I thought for certain that they misunderstood the question, so after the children sat down, I asked the teacher to repeat the question with additional words to clarify the ask – and once again, 75 percent of the class arose.

The lack of food and health care had quickly taken a painful and deadly toll. The teacher shared that some children were not able to arrive on time for school on a regular basis as they must first complete their long list of chores or tend to the needs of a sick family member. Some never attended school on Tuesdays and Thursdays. On these days, the children were needed to forage for food for the family.

We also began to understand why these children were constantly making every effort possible to collect our empty water bottles, which they called chupas. When an empty bottle was set down, multiple children aggressively reached out to secure it. They loudly clamored for these bottles as they reached through the barred windows of our small first-aid clinic.

We learned that when relatives, most often a grandmother or aunt, agree to assume care of these orphans, they often cannot feed these extra mouths. The chupas are worth a little sum of money, or they can be used as a bartering tool for small amounts of food. Children who return home with many chupas are rewarded with a bit of "extra" food that evening. This realization permanently changed the way I now see an empty water bottle. It is not a piece of plastic to just recycle. It is a very small, but very welcomed, additional nourishment for these hungry stomachs. No wonder so many little hands scrounged for these bottles.

The student interviews began. We asked the same questions of each child to learn more about their lives. Most of the children responded about living with an aunt or other relative, enjoying going to school, and wishing their mothers were still alive.

But one boy caught us by surprise. He responded quite factually and with no emotion as he answered the questions:

What is your family like? "My family? I have none."

What is your favorite thing to do? "Sit long and think hard."

If you had one wish, what would it be? "To die nicely with not so much hurting."

It was this last response that was suffocating to hear. My teammate needed to step outside to compose himself, his heart so full of hurt for these children. This boy had seen so much pain and suffering devour his own family, with slow and agonizing deaths from malaria, HIV/AIDS, dehydration, malnutrition, infections, and starvation. His one wish was to die nicely and he thought about that a lot. What did I wish for when I was in third grade? Surely it was not to die nicely.

Death, Death, Death
(written by a boy, age 15)

I fear to die because I saw my mother die,
I became annoyed and confused,
That is why I fear to die.
Death, Death, Death,
Death took both my parents,
They were not born rich,
They left me with poor relatives,
They mistreated me,
I still feel the suffering.
Death, Death, Death,
Each and every one of us knows that death is a bad thing,
For it separates us from those we love too soon.
We are orphans, stop mistreating us,
We are the younger generation of this world,
We just want to live, we just want to be happy.

Voices Deserving to be Heard

A few days after arriving in Africa for one trip, our team visited several local schools, at their request, and we were eagerly welcomed with open arms. Every stop was an eye-opening, gut-wrenching learning experience. The teachers and students asked for nothing, but their voices gave us much to consider long afterwards.

At one elementary school, the children were well-versed in their culture and history and sang deeply and passionately about how their parents had been brutally slaughtered years ago during a war and how those who survived fiercely fought to make a better, safer life for their children. They sang with great emphasis and emotional rawness about the deep pain of such great and sudden loss, wanting to make their parents and their teachers proud of them, feeling blessed for the opportunity to not be living in a war zone like their relatives had experienced, and abundantly thankful for the opportunity to be in school. Their family histories and heritage were extremely important to them, and these songs were their way of proudly preserving these stories and carrying their lessons learned from generation to generation.

The children also sang a song called the "Adam and Eve Apple Story," in which they theatrically enacted the biblical song's lyrics. Their message in this song was that we all make mistakes, which can be forgiven, and that we can and should always learn from our mistakes as well as forgive others their mistakes as we move forward in life. Even at their young ages, they actively practiced this in their own lives, and they shared examples of that with us.

They sang to us about the visitors from the United States of America and sang, "You are very welcome here!" Watching them dramatically sing and dance and act was both heartbreaking and mesmerizing at times. They were mature beyond their years in many ways. And they had such inherent natural talent. I often felt enveloped in their emotional outpouring, especially so in the manner in which they preserved and protected their history and respect for their ancestors.

Next, I met a young girl at the nearby secondary school. The school's headmistress asked me to spend some time with her as she had grown silent over the preceding week. Her teacher shared that this girl excels in every subject and works very hard on her studies when she is well enough to focus. She looked very thin, and she was feverish and wheezing. She also had a significant lack of appetite that seemed to be more related to her becoming accustomed to having little food to eat. Both her mother and father had recently died of AIDS-related complications. She lived alone. She had been tested and was on appropriate therapy.

We sat together on the school walkway and quietly talked. I gently held her hand. She asked if I could make her feel better. I explained I could not cure her HIV. She said, "No, I miss my mother. So now all I want is to feel a little better so that I can learn in school." That I could help her with, starting with a mutual big hug, my protein bars, some fruit, and my water bottle, all with the headmistress' approval. She said she hoped to become a nurse. This young girl lamented that her greatest sadness was that she would never bear a child of her own. She cried; I cried with her. But then she grabbed my shoulders and said, "Let us be brave and have hope." She was the braver one on that day.

In another village, we learned very few of the younger children living there attended school. Earlier that day, we traveled to the school closest to this village, and noted that the elementary classrooms were filled with children of mixed ages, from six to sixteen, in every grade level. A local school headmaster explained that several years ago, when the country's border opened to a neighboring country, people from that neighboring country crossed the border and abducted children as they walked through the thick vegetation in the farm fields on their way to school in the early morning hours. These children were taken across the border and sold into the child trafficking market.

Some mothers lost all of their children to the traffickers, and some, in their deep grief, committed suicide. We learned the local government stepped in to stop these egregious acts. The headmaster said the traffickers then started to pay people to retaliate by crossing the border and bringing back the heads of children. Children from the village were found along the river, on their path to school, violated like this. Frantic mothers began to refuse to send their children to school until they were older, able to run faster, and were beyond the prime age for trafficking. This explained the varying age span within any one classroom. According to the headmaster, the government had immediately and aggressively increased its efforts to negate the attacks with force and patrols, and the abhorrent behavior ceased. But the fear remained.

I asked the headmaster if this story as he told it was wholly factual, explaining that, to me, this was so very surreal. He assured me it was all true. I recalled how earlier that day, I walked into a first grade classroom just as the teacher was using a very explicit child trafficking poster to explain to these innocent ones exactly what this is and what they need to avoid. In her directness, she minced no words. Education on this topic was a serious top priority here. The children listened intently and, based upon the questions they asked, clearly understood her message.

At first, I could only listen as I struggled with absorbing what the teachers had said. No further words came just then. No outward reaction happened. Later, the numbness wore off and I greatly struggled to accept these revealed truths. I mourned for the families who tragically lost so much. I hesitated sharing this story, naively finding it unbelievable myself at first. I questioned my reticence, realizing I feared no one back home would believe such a story. "Tell the story," the Voice whispered. Yes, their voice, the one that was prematurely stolen from them, deserves to be heard.

Awareness is key. Community is key. Education is key. Love is the key. I overcame my temporary weakness, vowing to continue their fight and to tell their story. When truths such as these are shared with you, tell those stories when you return home. Be their voice.

How to Be a Responsible Youth
(written by a boy, age 14)

Oh Youth! Let's wake up!
To take decision – decision of our future.
Tomorrow is ours; we are the leaders of tomorrow.
Be disciplined, respect others.
Help the needy ones.
And never mistreat them, Oh Youth!

Respect yourself, Oh Youth!

Say "No" to diseases, avoid drug abuse,

And you will achieve a better life into tomorrow.

Zeto

As I addressed a group of nurses in the United States, giving a presentation about a recent trip to rural Africa, I heard myself say, "In this village, as is seen in similar villages throughout this African country, one in five children dies of malaria before the age of five." I looked up – not one person reacted to that statement about child mortality. I had failed miserably in getting the true message across. How easy it is to get caught up in statistical numbers. And how easy it is to not translate those statistics to real living, breathing people.

The next time I gave a presentation, I added less abstract examples of what I have witnessed. Suddenly, everyone in the room was listening as I spoke about Zeto.

He was sitting quietly in the sand, his tattered and too-small clothes barely covering any of his stick-thin body. I asked the young boy his name. He replied, "I have no name yet but I am called Zeto for now." I asked him why he has no name and he pointed towards his father, who was busy carving wood. "He will tell you," he replied. I sat down beside the boy's father, who shared that he earns fifty cents a day working fourteen-hour days, delivering supplies on his donkey cart. His donkey rested nearby, looking so thin and weak, with tufts of body fur missing. The father looked even more thin and more weak.

He went on to explain that this income enables him to buy small amounts of rice and sadza to keep his family alive. But when someone becomes ill, there is nothing left for medicine. With an unsteady voice, he said, "So the babies die because we have not even the few monies for malaria pills. Mothers wail with grief. Nothing can be done when the fevers come. We just wait to see what will be."

This gentle man continued speaking, "Our family name must be carried from generation to generation so that we are not lost, so that our children know their ancestry, their fathers and mothers, and before them, their fathers and mothers. Many die when babies. So for my son, he will not hold my family name until he is fully of the age of five years. If he lives until that age, he will be strong enough to fight malaria without the medicine. And God willing, he will live to carry forward the family name to his son. So what you ask, here is the reason for why we name our eldest son later in life, because of malaria, because of its smell of death and darkness."

As he continued to carve the wood, I stared at him in silence trying to absorb his story. I have attended many Western birthing events in which naming the baby was a joyous process. We perused baby name books, diligently researched meanings of names, and considered family history and traditional family names. Parents proudly proclaimed the baby's name even before the actual birth. Here in this village, the cherished family name was withheld from the oldest boy until he was five years old. It was withheld with apprehension every time the child was ill. It was withheld with the desperate hope that the child would survive the first five years of his life. It was withheld with the knowledge that a treatable illness can unexpectedly wipe that precious life from existence in a few short days.

I spoke with other villagers that morning. With sadness, they told the same story. It was heartbreaking to hear their stories of infant mortality. They spoke of the lack of insecticide-treated malaria nets. Some who had received the nets used them to cover and protect their animals, as they sorely needed them for food. Some stated that nets which were donated by nonprofit organizations were stolen and used for fishing or drying fish. One was stolen and used for a wedding dress.

I watched five young mothers, each holding an infant, sitting in front of our first-aid station waiting to speak with our medical staff. With a heavy heart, I wondered if all five babies would reach the age of five. Suddenly, the one in five dying before the age of five was embodied in the real living, breathing angelic faces before me. When a child's life could be saved by a five-dollar malaria net or by a few dollars in medication, delivering more mosquito nets to these families became a priority.

One in five before the age of five was no longer a statistic on a piece of paper. One in five now had a face. I gazed upon Zeto's handsome face and prayed that he remained healthy, alive at five, and that he would soon proudly bear his family name.

Life Is Like a Baseball Game

In my travels to rural Africa, I witnessed the after-effects of the deaths of so many young people. In many villages I saw the very young being raised by the very old – with very few people between the ages of thirty-five to sixty-five. The ravages of HIV/AIDS had devoured those people, leaving many orphans to be raised by elderly grandparents, aunts, or uncles. In situations where extended families did not exist, the orphans needed to fend for themselves.

After meeting Zeto's father, I repeatedly witnessed that in other villages children are not given a proper name until their fifth birthday. The explanation was always the same. Family names are names of honor to be carried on from generation to generation. I learned that in many parts of Africa, two in five children die before the age of five not just from malaria, but also from dehydration, severe diarrhea, starvation, HIV/AIDS, or other ailments. Treatment options exist in the world, but not for these people. Manual-pump water wells break with constant use, and no one can afford thirty dollars for repairs. So there is not always an adequate or reliable water supply for drinking or watering food gardens.

Painful dehydration symptoms plague the children, as they suffer seizures and fever in their final hours of life. Some wells are so contaminated the children develop horrible fatal illnesses that play out over painful days and weeks before death consumes these little ones. Some villages have no wells, and the women walk long distances to collect water from streams. Thirsty animals may seek water from those streams, which then become polluted with animal waste. A rainfall is greeted with children rushing to mud puddles and dropping down on all fours to scoop the muddy water into a piece of jagged edged plastic using a makeshift wooden spoon, to savor it for later in the day. Occasionally you might see a child putting his face in that mud puddle to take a drink, then wiping his mouth with his hand, and watching the streak of mud cross from his lips to his cheek. Death is constantly knocking on the door.

White blankets are among the most commonly requested items from many of the villagers I met. The first time I saw "white blankets" on a requested supply list, I asked, "Why? It is so hot here." An elder woman smiled at my innocence and directed my gaze to the oncoming procession of people. As they moved closer to us, I saw a small form wrapped in a white blanket. "Malaria," she solemnly and quietly said. "Sometimes we use mats, but are not white blankets more respectful to the dead? We cannot afford coffins." Sadness for these small angels who need to be clothed in white blankets enveloped me. I added "white blankets" to the needs list.

In another village, in the distance, I saw a young man who appeared to be digging a hole in the ground, as if he were planting a small bush or some crop. Wondering if he had the ability to plant a small community garden, I walked to where he was digging. Then I saw the tiny brown bundle off to the side, and I saw a young woman silently standing in the background with tears running down her face. I offered my condolences on the loss of their child. The mother explained that the baby contracted malaria. Her husband made a very paltry amount of money doing very harsh labor in the nearby fields. They could not afford what amounts to five dollars for medication. The entire family monthly income was less than ten dollars, and that amount could not be collected for another two weeks. The extremely harsh and painful truth is that people die for the equivalent of not having the money that elsewhere buys a large cup of some gourmet drink. When you are volunteering, thoughts like these will likely nag at your conscience during moments of emotional upheaval. You will need to make peace with your thoughts to be effective, and to turn those thoughts into action.

This mother's tears came from not being able to afford a clean white blanket in which to wrap her child for burial. As previously seen in other villages, people in this community could not afford wooden coffins, so they instead used white cloth, most often small blankets.

We had just come from the local church services and I was wearing a jacket that I had been given right before the trip. The morning weather was unusually cool. Originally, I did not pack this jacket, but on my way out the door of my home to begin the journey, I stopped and pulled it from my closet and tossed it my bag. Even as I did so, I questioned what I was doing. I knew it would be at least 90 degrees Fahrenheit there, and the dust from the dirt roads would render the new jacket a mess. But I felt oddly compelled to bring it with me. As it turned out, the African dirt was just the reason why this article of clothing was made. As I removed my new white jacket as an offering, this young woman and I exchanged a look that connected one mother to another mother. I felt her painful brokenness in my own mother's heart. We cried in unison. Sometimes all you can do is hug and pray and share the tears. And sometimes, that is all we are called to do.

As I walked away to allow them some privacy, I could hear the mother offer prayers of thanks for bringing this beautiful life to them for a short time and for the blessing of receiving this white garment just in time to lay her to rest. With more quiet sobs, I too gave silent thanks.

One very early morning in a different village, I was walking down a road and saw what looked like pieces of rags clinging to blood-soaked dirt near the edge of the road. Later that day, I learned from the overseer of the local church that a woman from the village had experienced sudden labor pains during the night. Her family was attending an event in a neighboring town and she was alone in her hut. Realizing that something was seriously wrong, she attempted to walk the four miles to the nearest medical clinic. She and her partially born baby did not complete their journey. They both died silently, painfully, and alone in the roadside dirt, in the darkness of night. I thought about the blood-stained dirt and what was likely part of her skirt. I fought back the nausea. My head hurt. My heart grieved for her and her child.

On a different trip, we visited a hospital nearest to a village where we were volunteering, almost an hour's ride away. The midwife employed there said that often women do not come to them for any health-care services until they are already in active labor because the government charges a fee for services provided at this facility. Women cannot afford the fee, and often they do not even know how prenatal care might help them and their growing babies. She said that the practitioners are not able to perform Cesarean section surgery at this facility, so if a mother needs surgery, they must send her home, with instructions to go to a hospital.

Knowing that most of the births there happen at night, I asked what happens then. She said that transport drivers will not come to these villages at night due to personal safety concerns, so the women need to wait until the next morning to get transportation to the hospital. They go home, in active labor, walking, or sometimes on the back of a bicycle, and do the best they can as their labor progresses. I asked again what that means – this time, she lowered her eyes and bowed her head, as she quietly said, "They and their babies die in their dark huts in great pain." There was nothing more either of us said right then, instead taking a solemn moment of silence for these women and their infants.

How does a volunteer process experiences like these? How does one keep her heart from shattering beyond repair when witnessing such deep pain and sorrow, not being able to fix everything that people look to you to fix? How do we make peace with these thoughts?

When I was a teenager, I played softball on a girls' team. I did a great deal of thinking during the many hours spent on that sports field. One day when I was playing first base, I looked out over the field as everyone warmed up for the game. It occurred to me that the game field was much like the game of life. So at the age of fourteen, I went home and wrote this analogy. With each passing year, I find it to hold true in my life.

Life is like a baseball game. We all start out in the dark protected dugout where there are not yet any expectations of us. When it is our turn, we are gently nudged or "pushed out" to home plate, and we start swinging. We hit the ball, run to first base, and once there we discover that twenty years have gone by. Being young and energetic, we do all we can to steal second base, sometimes running back to first base to tag up, then trying again. We make A LOT of mistakes. Some people never make it that far – sometimes we only bunt the ball, and things like childhood illnesses or tragic accidents stop us from even getting to first base. Sometimes we get hit on the head with a foul ball or strike out at the plate, or get cocky or overconfident and take a bad risk in trying to steal second base. So many things conspire to call us "out" and drive us back "home."

While on second base, we think "Could it possibly be forty years already? I am dusty, slower, hopefully wiser, and I am halfway home." We ponder about the shortstop on the baseline ahead. How do I get around that fifty-year midlife crisis looming in my path? And people all around us are hitting home runs or foul balls, dropping the ball, making errors in the field, cheering or booing – all of which affects us on that baseline. Sometimes we are looking for our buddy to pull out a home run for us, but instead they disappoint us and strike out, leaving us stranded on base. And it affects our actions – we may get too sure of ourselves, only to end up making an unforced error – and being penalized for that. We go from hero on one play to zero the next. We win, we lose a few, we sometimes need to go extra innings. But we know that the game must go on and we just can't stay on one base forever.

Well, we get past that shortstop, and then it seems like we fly to third base. Can it be sixty years already? We are getting tired from all of that running, and we see those youngsters on base behind us. What to do? Which direction to take?

Sometimes another illness or tragedy hits us, and we also are called home just then – the decision is made for us. Other times, we wait, then suddenly that third base coach is waving us home. We run with our eye on the reward, when we slide back into home and return to that dugout from which we began our journey. We know that we truly are "safe," and we rejoice with all of our family and friends who are there waiting to welcome us back to where we started our adventure. And whether we took the long road home or the short road, and whether we hit a home run or made many errors, He is there with a high five saying, "Good job, my child. Welcome home."

I remind myself to trust in our "Coach", for there we will find true peace. I tell the children who I meet in Africa to surround themselves with people who can be good coaches for them – who will understand and accept them for who they really are in their hearts, who will embrace the good and help them through the not-so-good. In Africa, there is a proverb that states, "He who loves you, loves your dirt." How very true is that.

I encourage the children to seek forgiveness when they fail, and offer forgiveness when someone fails them. And I encourage them to do what I think can be the hardest of all – forgive yourself. I tell the children to try to accept that there are some things that one cannot control. As an example, I ask them to circle their right foot clockwise. As they are doing that, I ask them to also now draw number six in the air with their right hand. Go ahead, try it!

Now while I know all of that might be good advice, I also know that it is easier said than done. But it is a goal I believe is worth striving for. For me, the key is to pray for understanding and clarity for what God wants me to be doing, and then to actually have the courage to do it. In the midst of sometimes seemingly nothing, in the midst of feeling lost and alone, as I witnessed in Africa, I found that I had everything if I held on to my faith, looked to my Coach for guidance as I round the bases to get back home, completing the circle of life.

AIDS, AIDS, AIDS
(submitted anonymously by a student)

AIDS is the most dangerous disease in the world,
It leads to the death of many people in the world.
Loss of weight and sunken eyes are signs.
AIDS leads to poverty among Africans and the world.
Playing with sex without using a condom
    when one of two people has the disease is deadly.
People in the world are crying and suffering greatly because of AIDS.
So my friend, be aware of AIDS with this warning:
Always be faithful, with one partner only.

Baba

I watched in wonder at the process for building a men's workshop in one village. What do you do when premade bricks do not exist? Well, first you drive your truck to the river and collect the silt. The silt is mixed

with cement and poured into handmade rectangular molds. Then you allow that to dry in the direct sun for several days. I quickly learned that
dropping one of these painstakingly handmade bricks will likely cause it
to break into several pieces. And when a team member lifted one of the
dried bricks and found himself staring at what a villager loudly warned
was a poisonous mamba snake, I gained immediate respect for the need
to use more caution.

The afternoon sun was blazing and the temperature rose to over 100
degrees Fahrenheit. Babandiishe was resting alone under a tree. I introduced myself and asked if I could join him. He smiled and shook my
hand with the traditional three part handshake. In the first part, you clasp
someone's hand as you would in the West; in the second part, both indi-
viduals lock thumbs while still clasping hands, so your thumb is pointed
upwards, and the handshake finishes by going back to the traditional
Western shake. He told me to call him Baba.

I asked Baba if his name had a meaning. He replied that it means head
of the house. He explained that the men's workshop would give him a good
place to labor as he tried to provide for his family by carving different items
out of wood. Baba explained that when his country had a larger influx of
visitors, he was able to sell his carvings in the open market. Political changes
removed that opportunity. As he talked about the many changes he had
seen in his life, he asked, "What do you think is the wooden carving most
often sought after now?" "Elephant," I said with confidence. "No," he replied. "Giraffe?" "No," he again replied, with his face now draped in a solemn
sadness. I was puzzled. "Hippopotamus?" I weakly offered.

He paused for several seconds, as if he was very much struggling to say
these words out loud, then haltingly, he whispered. "It... is... coffins."

My mind tried to wrap itself around his answer. Coffins? The implications
of his response immediately numbed my mind. Then I struggled to accept my
own comprehension of his words, as the truth settled in my conscience. Wood
was being harvested for coffins, not for carving wooden statues for sale, but
because the market demand for coffins was significantly higher.

I looked around and I reflected on the many stories the villagers had
recently shared with me. All five of the village wells had broken at the

same time. The forty dollars to repair them could not be raised. Children died painful deaths due to dehydration. The ground was parched due to lack of rain. In this long drought, crops shriveled into nothing. Even more children died, slowly and painfully, from starvation. Animals wandered away in search of food and would be found lying dead, some foaming at the mouth, where their fruitless journey ended. Goats licked the white paint from the exterior walls of the school building in a futile effort to find nourishment. In the darkness of night, elephants could be heard surrounding the village in search of maize and beans. At times, lions had been spotted in search of goats.

As seen so frequently in other villages, malaria's death grip latched on to so many children under the age of five due to lack of affordable antimalarial drugs. An African health-care worker once shared that malaria kills one African child every thirty seconds. HIV/AIDS took the lives of others due to inadequate continuous supplies of government-issued antiretroviral drugs. Food packs for those with HIV/AIDS formerly donated by nonprofit organizations no longer existed, making ingesting the antiretroviral therapy medications on an empty stomach very difficult. Tuberculosis also wielded its hand of death, especially so in the drug-resistant cases. Cholera infected many of the remaining water supplies and brought its own dark cloud with it. Childbirth could have its own complications. One man told me that when a mother goes to have her baby, the husband gets a child or a wife back, but often not both.

Families lived, or rather they survived, on fifty cents a day, which often was not nearly enough to sustain a healthy life for any extended period of time. Life expectancy for women in this village was in the mid-thirties. Men's life expectancy was a bit longer, but still only forty years of age.

And so coffin-making was flourishing. Baba dejectedly shrugged his shoulders as I asked him to confirm my reflections on this. "Quite true," he murmured, "All of it. Yes, all of it. And this, this death, makes my business grow and grow. It is sad, yes, but it is also the way of life here now. It is what it is, and it is what it will be without help from visitors or governments from outside. We have nothing here that the rest of the world wants. No diamonds, no gold, no oil. Who in this world will care for people like us? Who?" He threw his hands in the air in apparent acceptance of the despair and defeat that he had come to know so well. Then he continued with his coffin-making.

It is sad, yes. Gut-wrenchingly sad. Here among these beautiful people, the high probability of early death casts a giant shadow with the dawn of each new day because of where they were born. And coffin-carving flourishes. Oh, how I wish the demand for elephant carvings was the greater need!

As Baba watched me fight for composure, he gently touched my shoulder and said, "It is OK. We will come to the Promised Land, all of us, some sooner than others. And it will be OK. This is life." Through my quiet weeping, I knew that he was right. I prayed that I might see whatever it was that I was supposed to do to relieve the suffering that I was blessed to have just learned about from this strong man. My hands had more work to do, as did Baba's hands, that day. And if my hands were guided to success, maybe his hands could take a well-deserved rest.

Jewel

I was first introduced to Jewel Kilcher's music when my husband asked me to listen to her song titled "Foolish Games." He was drawn to the deep soulfulness and raw emotion in her voice. A short time later, I chaired a talent show at my son's elementary school. Two girls sang another song by this talented artist called "You Were Meant For Me," accompanied by their father on guitar. I watched as the audience seemed to hang on Jewel's lyrics, the older ones nodding as if they truly understood what was being conveyed. Soon after, my husband called me into our living room saying, "I want you to watch this video. It reminds me of you." The video was "Hands."

"Hands" is a single released from Jewel's album *Spirit*. The video begins with emergency responders working in what appears to be a natural disaster, maybe the aftermath of an earthquake. Jewel sees the crowd staring at the piles of rubble, while others just walk away. Some are digging in the rubble, searching for survivors, and Jewel joins those people. They rescue a man and three children. Although she is surrounded by chaos, Jewel remains calm and focused, and full of hope. As I watched the video and read the accompanying song lyrics, I hoped that one day my own hands would move more and more in that direction of kindness.

Flash forward eight years. With my children grown, I moved in that direction and began to volunteer in rural Africa. I fell in love with the people in the first country that I visited. No matter what I took there, no matter what projects we successfully completed, I was always gifted with the personal blessing of returning home more enriched and faith-filled from my experiences there. And although I had always believed that I grew up comparatively poor, I began to understand what real poverty is; what it is like to live in a war torn country; what it is like to be a woman living in a place with little respect for women's rights and sometimes their lives. I felt more and more drawn to committing time and resources to the people in these rural villages than ever before.

At one point, political upheaval in this African country made it unsafe for me to physically return. I continued to support the people in the village there as much as possible financially and with prayer from afar. In the interim, we took our team to another African nation and we did some very good work there.

But over time, these experiences also awakened me to the other side of this volunteer work that sometimes happens – the theft of money and goods, the inability to deliver true sustainable change, the demands for monetary bribes to get things done, prejudice, inflated egos, jealousies, confusing an intended hand up with a handout, power plays, and lack of accountability. I realized that some of my own well-meaning but naive approaches to projects may have inadvertently contributed to these problems at times.

I became disillusioned with this volunteer work, and wondered why it was so hard to do good. I internalized the experiences and made it about myself. I became selfishly lost in "me" and pushed away the invaluable lessons that I had learned from the great people of Africa.

One day as I was sitting at home alone and with a heavy heart, thinking about the great highs and several lows of the last several years of this volunteer work, and reflecting on my newly made decision to take a break from it all, the song "Hands" came on the radio. The person on the radio said, "Here is an old song for those of you who still believe in miracles."

As the song played, I heard Jewel sing:

> *If I could tell the world just one thing*
> *It would be that we're all Ok*
> *And not to worry 'cause worry is wasteful*
> *And useless in times like these.*
> *I won't be made useless*
> *I won't be idle with despair*
> *I will gather myself around my faith*
> *For light does the darkness most fear.*

But it was the second verse that found its mark in my heart:

> *Poverty stole your golden shoes*
> *It didn't steal your laughter*
> *And heartache came to visit me*
> *But I knew it wasn't ever after*
>
> *We'll fight, not out of spite*
> *For someone must stand up for what's right.*
> *Cause where there's a man who has no voice*
> *There ours shall go singing*

And that is when I could again clearly envision the people in rural Africa, the men, women, and children who have no voice. Those people from whom poverty had taken so much, yet who still had their joyous laughter. My heart began to sing again, to fight, not out of spite but because someone must stand up for what's right.

I felt my sadness dissipate as I reflected on the song's chorus. *While my hands are small, they are my own and I am never broken. For in the end, only kindness matters.* Those words stirred deeply in my heart: *In the end, only kindness matters.* The voice on the radio was right, for once again I was becoming the person who still believed in miracles. I wrote to Jewel to thank her for her inspiration, and while I never heard back from her, I hope that she somehow knows that her gift of music is such a blessing to many of us.

So now I had my new mission, and I was renewed with fresh energy. Thank heaven for such beautiful songs. Thank heaven for the voices who stand up for what's right. I prayed for the strength and guidance to be one of those voices. I felt my smile returning. And I knew that my laughter would soon follow.

Water Blessings

I was a sweaty, dirty mess. Temperatures in the village were near 100 degrees Fahrenheit for the entire work day. Our team depleted our water supply before day's end and we were becoming dehydrated. My skin was grimy and gritty and my hair was greasy.

As we drove back to our rooms for the evening, I wondered if we would be blessed with running water at the end of this busy day. That was a constant unknown on a daily basis in this African town. As I unpacked our supplies, I heard two team members very joyously announce that the water was working.

We raced to get showers. The water was very cold but I was so thankful that it was streaming and wet and clean. I quickly lathered in soap and shampoo. Water gushed from my shower nozzle. Then suddenly it turned to slow drips. I turned the faucets and nothing happened. They just kept loosely spinning. Soap was drying on my skin. Shampoo streamed down my face and into my eyes. I deduced that the solution was to turn those rusty faucets handles even more and even harder.

The faucet pulled completely out of the wall, leaving a large ragged gaping hole in the plaster, and breaking the rusty water pipe within that wall. But then, the water began to gush from this broken pipe! I started to call for help, as it quickly rose over my ankles. Then I looked at all of that free-flowing water. So instead of calling for help, I giddily continued to rinse off the soap and wash my hair.

Soon I heard a frantic knock at my door. "Are you OK?" a team member asked. I had already reasoned that we could fix the pipe and wall later. So I ignored the call and continued to enjoy my modified shower.

The knocking at the door grew louder and more rapid. "Hey, a bunch of soapy water is pouring out from under the door of your room." I thought, "OK, well, yes, that might be a problem."

I stepped out of the shower and quickly dressed. My room had begun to flood and the water indeed made a beeline to the door. I explained what happened and soon we had people fixing the ruptured pipe.

Of course, everyone noticed that I had taken the time to finish my shower instead of seeking immediate help. And I found out that when the pipe in my room broke, while I had gushing water, three other team members suddenly had no water in their showers. I did feel a twinge of guilt!

After the cleanup, and after dealing with a pesky scorpion that made his home outside of my door, we joked about the water situation and how I chose to handle it. But we also seriously discussed this great blessing of water: good, clean water. Life-giving water is the most basic and most precious commodity. We talked about the children we have seen on trips who run outside carrying little spoons when it rains. They scoop up water from the mud puddles and, spoonful by spoonful, they start to fill small containers. This water is later used for cooking the family's dinner. We talked about the very sick people we have met whose sole water supply is contaminated by the wandering animals who pollute it, resulting in serious waterborne diseases. We talked about infants and small children in the village who died of dehydration when all of the wells were broken. Can you imagine watching your child die because you had no way to hydrate him?

We talked about seeing young girls and women in the village where we were volunteering walk three or more miles to get water every day, starting at three in the morning and repeating that several times a day. So much of their day, every single day, is consumed with walking to a well, and then pumping and carrying water back to their huts. This is time that is not spent in school, not growing food, and not spent earning an income.

We talked about the women who carry this water in five-gallon yellow plastic containers called jerry cans. Someone noted that a jerry can full of water weighs almost forty pounds. No wonder these women have chronic neck and back problems! I have tried several times to lift one of these plastic containers full of water to the top of my head, mimicking what these women do. To date, I have never been able to lift it higher than my chin. If it ever does make it to my head, surely I would never be skilled enough to then walk miles like that, and with a baby swaddled on my back. I so admire the strength and fortitude of these women.

The next day, I walked into an elementary school room in a remote village. The teachers and students did not know that we were coming that day. On the blackboard, I saw drawings that were meant to teach the children how to go to the bathroom in the school's outdoor cement latrine, aiming carefully into the latrine floor's rectangular openings, known as "squat holes." Next to this lesson, I saw these words written in big letters: "We like to play football. We are lacking water. God help us."

The lack of access to clean drinking water is a major contributor to poverty. When I return to my own home, I marvel that when I turn on the kitchen faucet, abundant water flows forth. When I shower, I am often amazed at the seemingly endless stream of water that flows from the showerhead and that I can easily make the water temperature hot or cold. I listen to the sound of the machine that washes the red dirt, sand, or mud from the clothes that I wore on a trip. I can easily flush a toilet, water the flowers, and boil water to use for cooking dinner or for making tea. The water is pure and uncontaminated, and just appears simply by my turning a faucet right in my own home. I pray for the guidance to use these gifts wisely and to continue to find ways to offer assistance to those in such desperate need of basic resources in this world. I give thanks for those angels of mercy who labor so hard to bring clean drinking water to those in need.

I vowed to never take the blessing that flows from my kitchen faucet or my shower for granted. When you return home from your own trip to rural Africa, you may experience a new appreciation for basic comforts such as running water. Others around you may show little interest in your newfound enthusiasm. Learn to be comfortable with that. But continue to raise awareness using your personal experiences. At some point, the right person will hear your words and want to learn more.

The Boy

Angelina was HIV positive and suffered from recurring eye infections. She was a beautiful child with captivating dark brown eyes. Angelina's parents had died from AIDS-related complications and her elderly grandmother was now her caregiver.

We attempted to treat the infection at our small first-aid clinic. Angelina looked so tiny, so fragile. Yet she never complained, never made a sound as we cleaned and dressed her open wound. A few days later, Angelina and her grandmother returned to the clinic. We realized that at this point, advanced treatment for this eye infection was needed.

Later that day, we drove Angelina to the nearest hospital for more advanced and effective treatment. The nurse at the hospital explained that the doctor would not return for three more days. The hospital employed only this one physician, as all of the other clinicians had left this country in hopes of finding better working conditions and regular pay. As we debated if anyone at the facility could help Angelina before Monday, I noticed movement in what I at first thought was an empty hospital bed in a patient room next to where we were standing.

I could see the dust particles floating about the room in the narrow stream of light that filtered through the partially closed window blind. I saw an emaciated little boy sitting on the bed, and moving his left hand methodically up and down. He could not have been more than five or six years old. His skin was dry and flaky. Patches of his hair were missing. His limbs were stick-like, and I could see his bones protruding under his skin.

I looked more closely and saw that he was actually sitting very closely beside a woman and patting her on her back. He was lovingly comforting his mother, who was lying totally motionless and face down on the mattress. She was skeletal and deathly ill herself. She was alive, but appeared to be lifeless. He seemed to know that soon he would be yet another orphan.

I asked what would happen to him. The nurse said they are used to dealing with this situation and would figure that out when the time came. I wanted to help. The nurse said there is nothing that I could do, that this is the reality of life here. She asked that I not break the boy's concentration as the child was doing what he needed to be doing in that moment. I took one long last look – he was just a tiny little heartbroken boy. I prayed for some comfort for both of them.

Angelina stayed with nearby relatives for the next three days. We provided food for her care and funds for her upcoming doctor's visit and treatment. I thought about her often, but it was the boy who was permanently seared into my memory. My own little boys ran and laughed and played with their mother. This little boy, equally as precious as my very own, was his mother's guardian as she breathed her last breath. To this day, I can still see him sitting so upright on that thin plastic mattress, looking blankly ahead as he mindlessly but gently patted her back. He had to let go of her, but I have not been able to let go of him and I hold him in my prayers. Sometimes I wish I could wrap all of these hurting children up in my arms and take them home with me and shower them with abundant love.

Mother
(written by a boy, age 13)

Mother, the only God on Earth,
I love you Mum,
But the bad thing Mum,
Is that you are nowhere to be seen.
And I am just miserable left here on Earth.
God, help me in the darkness.
Make me to be seen not just as an orphan, because I am alone at sea.
Mum, where are you?
Most times I think I am dreaming,
I feel so bad minus seeing you.
Mother you risked your life when you were producing me,
A lot of pain and suffering at that time,
And I will never forget you.
Mother, are you there, really?
When I sleep, I dream of you.
Because you gave me parental love as much as possible,

Because when you cared after me, you were a good mother.
Mother, the Earthly God,
You are so sweet, lovely and nice,
But you now rest in peace.
May your soul always rest in peace.

Movie Night

When our team can find a power source, we often host a movie night for the children. Frequently, using electricity is not an option, but we have been successful in using generators with diesel fuel or solar power. The children absolutely love watching movies.

On one volunteer trip, using a new donated laptop/projector, we invited the older schoolchildren to watch "Invictus," the story of Nelson Mandela's efforts to increase national unity using South Africa's rugby team, a stirring film that I highly recommend. As the movie started, my teammate looked at me and said, "I never realized how much Nelson Mandela looks like Morgan Freeman." Well, we all had a good laugh, because the character of Mandela was actually being portrayed by Morgan Freeman. Our teammate thought this film was a real-life documentary, and we all enjoyed the good-natured teasing in that moment. The children sitting nearby also respectfully chuckled along with us.

The secondary school students deeply immersed themselves in Mandela's teachings. As the movie progressed, they nodded with approval at his thoughts and reasoning related to peace and unity. When the national anthem played during the movie's rugby match, they all stood up with hands placed over their hearts. They applauded Mandela's ability to forgive, to unite his people, to persevere. They were quietly absorbed in thought as the rugby team visited Robben Island, where Mandela spent eighteen years in jail, breaking rocks at a limestone quarry for much of that time. They stood and loudly cheered for the South African rugby team to win, as if they were actually watching the game in real time. They were on the edge of their seats as the ball moved down the field with each new play. They high-fived each other when their team ultimately won.

The movie ends with Mandela's car driving away from a sports stadium. Mandela is watching the celebration from his car, and his solemn voice is heard reciting "Invictus," a poem by William Ernest Henley. Invictus is a Latin word meaning "unconquered." The students listened intently, absorbing the power of the words.

The headmaster said that he received many requests to view the film again and as soon as possible. He did just that and invited the students' parents too. Watching the children absorb the lessons of Madiba, his clan name by which many Africans affectionately call him, with growing maturity and personal understanding of affliction and redemption, deeply touched us all.

People in many of the villages in which I have had the privilege to spend time express great love and respect for Nelson Mandela. The more that I experience in Africa, the more I understand why.

This encounter was not my first regarding the significance of this particular poem. A few years prior, on a very hot and sunny morning, our team and the village health-care aides we supported headed out on foot to the outskirts of a different village to conduct home visits. We found a very elderly man who had no living relatives, for they had all died of HIV/AIDS years ago. He was all alone in a small, remote hut.

This man was covered in excrement, too weak to walk, emaciated from lack of food, extremely dehydrated, and too weak to help himself in any way. He slowly lifted his head and looked up when we walked in. He mustered a very slight smile, and weakly said a few words in his native language, which our interpreter said translated to "Alleluia, God is good." His voice was raspy and he seemed to be confused, likely in part from the dehydration. He seemed to have been there in that stark condition for a long time. He had lost track of time, but he thought that many, many days had passed since he had fallen down on the dirt floor.

Our health-care aides helped him to bathe while I ran back to our base camp to find a change of clothes for him. When I returned, he changed into the new clothes, and soon he was looking clean and fresh. His concentration seemed to be returning. His torn and ragged clothes had been hand-washed and were hanging on a tree to dry. The aides assisted with moving him to the outside of his hut to feel the warm sunshine on his face and to breathe the fresh air. I watched him grasp a cup of tea with shaking hands, and happily savor each sip of the warm liquid while he took small bites of crackers. He was smiling big smiles now.

I sat alone against a nearby tree absorbing this depth of faith and how that faith somehow gave these wonderful people in this village hope, helping them to choose good, healing them, and sustaining them through adversity – great adversity.

A middle-aged man from this village sensed my internal conflict and sat next to me. This man said he had lived in South Africa some time ago and that he had learned much from the life example set by Madiba. He admonished me, saying, "Mama, wipe the tears. This man has been saved. Do you know the poem that Madiba said to his prisoners when he was in jail for so long in Robben Island? It is written by a man named Henley. Mr. Henley had a very poor life and he had tuberculosis, a disease we have here too. He had his leg cut off when he was only seventeen and it was very painful. Then right after, he was told the other leg would come off. He found a new doctor named Lister and he had surgery, but kept the foot. While in the hospital recovering, he wrote a poem called 'Invictus.' It means unconquered. It is about picking yourself up, no matter what you have done or did not do, and taking good charge of your life without excuses." Then he stood up and with pride, cited the poem so eloquently:

"Out of the night that covers me,
Black as the pit from pole to pole,
I thank whatever gods may be
For my unconquerable soul.

In the fell clutch of circumstance
I have not winced nor cried aloud.
Under the bludgeonings of chance
My head is bloody, but unbowed.

Beyond this place of wrath and tears
Looms but the Horror of the shade,
And yet the menace of the years
Finds and shall find me unafraid."

And then he proclaimed the final verse more loudly and with great passion:

"It matters not how strait the gate,
How charged with punishments the scroll,
I am the master of my fate:
I am the captain of my soul."

Then he reached down and gently patted me on the head and said, "Let others do what they will do, but you only trust in our God and He will show you how to be a good captain. Your duty is to not feel sorry or pity for someone like this man, but to help him be the master of his fate, with God's direction." As he walked away, I continued to reflect on this teaching. I did not verify the man's story about the inspiration for that poem as it never mattered to me. His lesson alone was a powerful one and it left a lasting impression on me.

This man spoke to me about survival and courage when we are faced with a test of adversity, and holding on to our faith and dignity regardless of whatever indignity may befall us. Indeed, I am responsible for steering my own ship. My choices, my decisions, my thoughts, my actions all determine if I am a good captain or not. I need to remember that with God's breath in my sails and His love in my heart, I am the master of my fate; I am the captain of my soul.

When you are volunteering in a place such as this, always remember to act with respect and treat people with the utmost dignity. Learn how to be a good captain.

PART III

Planning for Success: Practical Advice to Maximize Your Trip Experience

As a volunteer traveler to remote parts of Africa, your success could depend on your own pretrip preparation. Physical challenges such as malaria-carrying mosquitos, cholera exposure, and weather extremes may await you. Local convenience and hardware supply stores are often nonexistent. Lack of electricity, running water, and internet connection may catch you off guard. Your team may start out strong, but somewhere along the way, personal issues or conflicts may arise, threatening the group's cohesiveness. Airlines have limitations on the dimensions and weight of checked baggage, and at times, carry-on bags as well, all of which can incur additional and unexpected fees if exceeded. Being prepared to handle the challenges is a key to reducing stress and minimizing problems like this during your trip.

At times, you may think you have little to offer as a volunteer. But I can assure you that each of us has something to offer, and much to learn. Some basic programs and projects are a great way to begin to embed yourself in cultural exploration. Choosing the right organization to partner with is paramount in achieving a successful and meaningful trip.

As you consider whether a particular volunteer experience is a good fit for you, talk to people who have gone before you. The following thoughts and stories are insights which I have shared with new volunteers. These are also good narratives for any of us to reflect upon.

Deep Introspection: Why Do You Really Want to Go to Africa?

Prior to my decision to volunteer in Africa, certain experiences caused me to pause and reflect on my personal beliefs. One such event unfolded many years ago when I was eleven years old.

I grew up in a small coal-mining town in Pennsylvania. My parent's lives were often difficult, with Dad laboring in the coal mines and Mom working for the garment industry as a seamstress. Food staples were limited primarily to potatoes, cabbage, onions, canned soup, eggs, and buttered macaroni. People hunted during permitted seasons to put meat on the dinner table. Seeing a deer hanging on a tree in your yard during hunting season was always a good thing. For some families, meal portions were small and seconds were usually nonexistent. We had coal stoves in our kitchens but at times we could not afford the very coal that our fathers mined each day.

In the winter, thick ice coated the inside of the windows in our house, which was purchased on a payment plan by my parents from Sears and Roebuck for $700 in 1946. The house had no insulation, so we would stuff old rags and newspaper into the seams of the windows and doors, and then staple thick plastic to the inside and outside of the windows. This provided minimal protection from the harsh winters we often experienced in the mountains. Some days, the temperature in our house was so cold that when I awoke, I could see my breath. Shivering, I would quickly dress under the mound of blankets covering me. Then I headed to the kitchen and sat in front of the coal stove as I consumed generic rice cereal with diluted evaporated milk. We had outhouses, but at times, no toilet paper. I remain appreciative of those 400-plus paged department store catalogues that arrived in the mail several times a year, as they eventually made their way to the outhouses in lieu of toilet paper. We bathed in grey metal tubs in the kitchen, with water heated on the coal stove. We had no health or dental insurance. Few people had cars. My mom frequently worked two to three jobs to keep us afloat.

One day I returned home from my Saturday morning house-cleaning job, and my mother was in panicked tears. She had just received a letter in the mail notifying us that our gas and electricity were being shut off. We owed $27.43 and she did not have it. We barely had any food in the cabinet, and she already had an unpaid tab at the local grocer. I had just pocketed $2.50 from my three-hour-long house-cleaning job; however, I had already used it for some much-needed school supplies. The unpaid bill lay on the kitchen table as she reached into her coat pockets and emptied the contents – just a few coins. She bitterly laughed as she said, "Well, we have exactly forty-three cents. Where in God's good name are we going to find the other twenty-seven dollars by tomorrow?"

I kept our family Bible in my bedroom. It was one of the very few books that we owned. I often read passages and studied the colorful pictures. This Bible was published close to the year of my birth. I uncannily felt drawn to that book just then. When I picked up the Bible, the pages fell open to the book of Matthew. To my amazement, there I found exactly twenty-seven dollars – in crisp new bills. My Mom and I could not believe it.

I walked the three miles to town to pay that utility bill, in great wonder, thinking about God's good name that she had invoked. When I returned home, the Bible was still on my bed, opened to that same page. This is what I read at the top of the page, under the title of "Power of prayer": Matthew 7:7-8 "Ask, and it shall be given to you; seek, and you shall find; knock, and it shall be opened to you. For everyone who asks, receives; and the one who seeks, finds; and to him who knocks, it shall be opened."

This is a true, unembellished story and I sheepishly admit that I looked in that Bible a few more times afterwards during difficult financial times. While no additional funds were ever found there, my joyous faith-filled journey into the world of blessings and miracles had begun. My desire to learn from others and to use my own blessings to help others in need burned deeply. And yet unknown to me at that time, my future journeys to Africa were waiting for me.

As you explore and work through your desire to volunteer in Africa, delve into your motivation for that. Often it is rooted in your personal life experiences.

A Mistake is a Great Teacher
(written by a boy, age 15)

A trip to paradise (success) is not as sweet as paradise itself,
But when you fall down, try standing,
Always, even if standing seems too hard.
Learn the hard way.
A trip to paradise needs courage, energy and determination,
Sacrifice and commitment with the first fall will take you to paradise,
Success and failure are both hard worked for,
But the difference is the kind of materials that you use.
Reject of regret is doing the right thing in the right place at the right time.
Do that – and find paradise.

Persecuted Children: Emmanuel's Story

While volunteering in Africa, you may encounter practices and customs that are very foreign to you. These may be difficult for you to reconcile in your mind. Emmanuel's story is my example of that.

My teammate and I were asked to visit the huts where a family of eight lived, as one of their children was quite ill. A young mother in this family had three children. She and one of the boys, Emmanuel, were albinos. We were asked to deliver powdered formula, physician-prescribed medication, some basic supplies, and food. The formula was a special physician-recommended enriched formula used for children who showed a failure to thrive and were unable to breastfeed.

Accompanied by two trusted locals, we drove a long distance into the African bush. When our jeep came to a spot where it could no longer pass, we walked the remaining distance. We walked and walked, passing no one, hearing only the sound of birds singing. We discovered fresh peppermint growing along the path, and collected some to make tea. When we arrived at this family's home, we found the child was indeed quite ill and had been so for several days. His mother was holding him close to her body, as if she felt the need to protect him from us. He was wrapped in a blanket and we could only see his eyes and nose. Initially she would not look up at any of us and she kept her own face and head covered with a large shawl. We would need to earn her trust. I soon understood why.

The family members began to share some of what they experienced on a regular basis. We were told that they did not seek medical care in the nearest town for any reason. We learned that some people in the world believe that body parts of albinos have magical powers. Sometimes albinos are hunted down and dismembered or killed to obtain those body parts. Albino hair and limbs were used in potions and witchcraft rituals, in which prosperity, good health, or great wealth are guaranteed to the receiver of these potions. Some people are willing to pay several thousands of dollars for this concoction. That is why this family lived in such an isolated location. They desperately hoped to survive undetected by those who might try to harm them.

I told the boy's mother we brought a special formula for her son and that a doctor in town had asked us to deliver it to her. She unwrapped her son from the blanket and allowed us to see him. I watched my teammate speaking in Swahili as she demonstrated to the mother how to measure and count the teaspoons of powdered formula into the correct amount of water that had first been boiled, then cooled, and to then mix and feed that to her sick child. I saw this mother begin to respond, and to intently listen, then try this herself. I looked in amazement at this child. He was beautiful in every way. How could anyone ever want to cut off his arm or leg? And with a machete?

I opened a large container of peanut butter and sat down on an old thick log. A few of the men from this family joined me. They had never tasted peanut butter before and they relished the large spoonfuls that I shared with them. One of the family members told me that when an albino dies, he cannot be buried in the ground because people will dig him up and steal his bones. So this family, and many like them, lived far away from the madding crowd. They rarely traveled into town to get supplies for fear of being followed back to their homes. They never sought any external assistance for fear of exposing themselves as "ghost people." They never felt safe.

At first, I could not fully comprehend their stories. I had to force myself to concentrate on their words. I had to look into their eyes to know that these stories were true. Their eyes burned with these truths. This was done to someone because he has no pigment in his eyes, hair, and skin? That is his crime? A crime punishable by such brutality? And who are these people who pay enormous sums of money, more than $75,000, for human body parts and potions?

We provided them with some basic needs and medicine for the child, in addition to more powdered formula. We explained how additional formula would continue to safely be delivered to them after we departed. Later, we donated bicycles to this family and to others in this similar situation so that when they did need to make that dangerous trip into town for supplies, their journey could be made more quickly.

Even today, several years after this experience, there are times when I watch a fair-haired child riding a bicycle and I envision this little boy in Africa who will never go to school, never leave his home, always live in fear of being viciously attacked by another human. The mother in me silently cries for him and for all children who are hunted. Hunting children? This is something with which I will never make peace. I do not know what ultimately happened to Emmanuel and his mother, but my hope is that they have found some comfort and peace of mind in their lives. Living with that kind of constant fear and anxiety is extremely taxing on the individual and his or her family.

As I walked back to our vehicle, the lyrics to an old Michael Jackson song popped into my head. He sings about healing the world and making it a better place by caring for the living and being God's glow, which in turn will allow us to see that our world is heavenly and can shine again in grace.

I vowed to continue the fight to make the world a better place, even if it is just a very tiny part of the world. You may encounter witchcraft practices such as this one. Take the time to learn what is happening, wrap your head around the reality that it is still happening today, and assess if you can help even one person who is being persecuted. Each volunteer can do something, just one thing, to make a better place. Each of us can be God's glow for someone.

Easy Asks and Hard Questions

As a volunteer in rural Africa, you may find yourself in the company of some very sick people. Sometimes they will ask you very direct questions. Sometimes they will present you with a simple request. Researching the area of any country that you plan to visit in advance of arriving there is always a good idea. That often helps a volunteer to be more prepared for the types of situations or questions that might be posed to him or her. The following are examples of situations that I have encountered as a volunteer.

One day, our team sat with a small group of village men and women who were HIV positive. They walked about ten miles to the nearest clinic every month but they never knew if their medication would be available when they arrived. Sometimes they were told the supply ran out and the clinic would advise them to try again next month. They spoke slowly and sadly of their feelings of isolation and fear. When I asked how I could help, they replied, "If we could have a blanket that would be quite good. Even in the heat, our bodies feel cold." I reached out to touch the hand of the person next to me. Although the air temperature was quite warm, his hand felt ice cold. I covered his hands with the warmth of mine, and he smiled as he raised his eyes to meet mine.

We provided them with peanut butter and bread to supplement their minimal food supplies and promised that a blanket would be supplied soon. At the end of the meeting, we stood up to offer a warm embrace. Each of them held us in a tight embrace. One woman smiled through her tears and said, "Thank you for touching me. I had forgotten what that felt like." And I had forgotten what abundant power lies within the basic human touch. I moved that reminder to the forefront of my thinking: Remember, hugs heal.

We visited a man who was in his final days of battling an AIDS illness. He asked for a blanket to keep his fragile body warm, and for a potato. A blanket and one potato – that is all it took to bring him great comfort and peace in all of his bone-searing pain. He smiled broadly as he slowly savored the boiled potato and said, "Ahh, now I am very, very happy. This is all that I need."

Over the years, our team members coordinated an adult education day for the women in several African villages. We awaited their arrival, eager to learn from them, and they arrived, eager to learn from us. We taught classes in health and hygiene, malaria, HIV/AIDS, dehydration, cultivation and nutritional use of moringa trees, fire safety, first-aid, small business skills, use of the color wheel for nutrition, crafts and other projects as sustainable income sources, and yoga to strengthen the shoulders, necks, and backs of these women who carry such heavy loads on their upper bodies. We always allotted time at the end of the day for open discussion and questions.

As we returned to the villages and built upon these programs, the women grew to know us, and we grew to know them. We laughed together as we exchanged life stories. As this trust blossomed, the question-and-answer session became a more integral part of the training. During the first few sessions, we received questions such as:

Can we do more yoga next time?

Tell me again how much water I should try to drink every day?

How can I tell if my child has malaria, or something else, if he has a temperature?

If I find a bump in my chest, what does that mean? What should I do?

When a woman is breastfeeding her baby, does that keep her from getting with child again?

Were you sincere that I can eat the leaves of that tree (moringa) for vitamins and minerals?

What is a virus?

Is AIDS really caused by a virus?

Can you get HIV by eating from the same food of someone who is HIV positive? Or by sharing the same cup of drink?

You said the virus is passed in blood. We share sewing needles when we pierce our ears. Sometimes there is some tiny blood drops from the piercing. We cannot get HIV from the piercing needle, that is correct, yes?

Can I get HIV from kissing someone who has tested positive? What about hugging someone?

Were you ever tested for HIV? Does it hurt? Were you frightened?

Why do you want to help us? (Be sure that you have thoroughly answered this question BEFORE you engage in any volunteer trip.)

In each of the following years, the questions evolved into some very serious discussions, such as:

If my husband works away from home and I think he has been unfaithful to me while he is away, how do I protect myself from HIV infection when he returns home – without it becoming a violent encounter?

Can you help us to get medication for our HIV/AIDS? We make the long walk to the government hospital for the free medication but many times they have run out and they do not know when, or if, more will arrive. What can be done for us to live? Can you send us medicine from your country?

How do we teach the children with no parents about the dangers of violence and bad people who will promise them good things then use them in bad ways? Orphans will not remain alone for long if no one steps forward to help them. Someone always finds them and takes them away. Then they are gone forever. That is not good. Who can fix that for these children?

And then later:

I am getting married in just a few weeks. My husband-to-be is HIV positive and I am HIV negative. I have been taught by my tribe that if I "marry from the heart" (which she demonstrates by curling her fingers into the shape of a heart and places them on her chest), then I cannot become HIV positive from him. Is that true? I want to believe that. I need to believe that. Can you agree with that, Mum?

On other trips, I have seen the most troubling continuation of an old myth still being perpetuated – the belief that having a sexual encounter with an African virgin will cure HIV in a man who is HIV positive. I met an African "healer" who told me that he has advised men to do this to cure their AIDS. He believes that the young girl's "pure" blood will clean the virus from the infected person. He stated that men from all parts of the world, and sometimes an entire busload of men from foreign countries, have paid large sums of money to travel to African villages to "cure their AIDS" this way. "Today?" I asked. "Yes, of course today, and tomorrow too," he replied. He added, "Then they may go on safari."

I could not wrap my mind around the calmness with which this was stated, but I felt every fiber of my being contract in heart-wrenching sorrow for these young, innocent girls. As a volunteer, these are the kinds of experiences for which you need to be prepared.

AIDS
(submitted anonymously by a student)

AIDS, AIDS, such a killer disease,
Has left many children orphans, without parents.
Today people are crying because of AIDS,
What a terrible disease is this!
AIDS, AIDS,
Have you come to mop the world
Of boys and girls who do not care or pay attention,
But think only of love for pleasure?
Boys and Girls – THINK! Be wise. Be responsible.

Shackles and Chains

While traveling as a volunteer, you will likely visit local African historical sites. Some of the ones that I have visited in Africa house chilling stories.

The beginning of this story is a happy one indeed. Our team had been working hard in rural East African villages. Some of our work needed to be delayed due to our supplies being trapped for an extended time in a shipping container that needed to clear customs. We received a very generous offer of an overnight exploration to a nearby island, and we gratefully leaped at the opportunity to learn more about life in another part of Africa.

Our tour led us through a city maze of narrow alleys on a hot muggy day. My eyes widened in excitement as I absorbed the crowded marketplace overflowing with tables of produce and spices, the winding labyrinth of streets lined with beautiful unique merchandise, the smell of fresh cashews, and the history of many years gone by.

We oohed and aahed over the elaborately carved wooden doors which adorned houses and hotels. Our guide stated that many years ago, the local rulers had slaves create these masterful works of art, and many of these doors represented a sign of wealth and status in the community. I marveled at the intricate details in the beautiful floral and geometric designs. I turned my attention back to our guide just as he was explaining that, to assure the artistry on certain doors would not be replicated, the hands of the slaves who made them were cut off.

That stopped me in my tracks. Surely I had misheard or misunderstood. I looked to him for confirmation, hoping for a retraction, but instead he said, "Yes, it is true, it happened here. The sultan (ruler) was able to boast that he had the grandest door of all time." Suddenly, the wooden doors smelled like death to me. Suddenly, they represented the deepest darkness in this world. I mourned for those craftsmen and for what they endured so that their work would live on as a unique material possession symbolizing pride and wealth. The bustle of the city around me seemed to quiet as my heart filled with pain and sadness for their suffering. I could no longer look at this door as a thing of beauty.

Our tour guide ushered us into a white wooden building which appeared to be a church, and we descended down the steps into the cellar. I thought, "What is this cold, dark, claustrophobic space?" He explained that this is where the slave trade flourished and that we were standing in what had been the "holding pen" for slaves on "market day." Rusty chains and thick metal shackles used to tether slaves were still attached to the cracked stone walls. Initially, I heard people talk about how the slaves were given no food, no water, no fresh air. But within minutes, all talking ceased as we all began to grasp the enormity of what had happened in this chilling place.

Oh my gosh! Oh My Gosh!! OH MY GOSH!!! In the few minutes that it took to walk through this dungeon, with its low roof and the haunting silence in the air, the air felt poisonous and I struggled to breathe. The reality that many thousands of people were "stored" here and then sold, the brutality of that, the lack of any concept of humanity and decency, the total disrespect for life, hit me in waves of nausea. Standing there, I tried to imagine those who were held there and what might have been some of their deep, searing pain, their indescribable emptiness and sadness, their abandonment of any hope. Pictures do not do justice to the tragedies that happened there. Actually stepping into the footprint of what these people endured is a gripping experience that one never forgets. And should never forget.

We learned about the efforts of missionary and explorer David Livingstone and others who worked endlessly to abolish slavery. Yet it was not until the late 1800s that this was realized.

Our guide explained that a church was built on this slave market site with the altar positioned over the location of the whipping post. He said slaves were lined up and tied to a tree and whipped. The ones who did not cry or pass out sold for higher prices as they were labeled as "extra strong." More cruelty. More suffering. More pain. I slowly turned to the altar and forced myself to think about that whipping post. Prayer after prayer for those people streamed from my consciousness. Tears for them, and especially for those who did not cry for themselves, soaked my face. What was I to take from this experience of suffering and cruelty? I felt so shaken.

I thought about a quote I heard some time ago, which was attributed to Albert Einstein. "Nothing that I can do will change the structure of the universe. But maybe, by raising my voice I can help the greatest of all causes – goodwill among men and peace on Earth." Yes, I needed to speak up and share these experiences with others.

Later that day, the sky darkened and torrential rains fell. I was dripping wet, yet I felt no relief from the heat of the day. My mind could not release the dark images of what I had just seen on this emotional roller-coaster ride. But I could go forward and raise my voice to tell their stories, hoping that history will not always repeat itself. As a volunteer, you may be asked to raise your voice. That is not always an easy thing to do. Do it anyway.

Just a Word
(written by a boy, age 13)

When dogs encounter,
They bark, stop, sniff, then move apart,
When birds encounter,
Their sound of music fills the air,
One by one with great flare.
Even cups in a tray make noise as they are touched,
Yet the human voice is often hushed.

Hairy Beasts

You will encounter many animals while visiting Africa. Some are exotic. Some are odd looking. Some are enormous in size. In your travels, use caution when in the presence of these animals. Many of them are dangerous.

While enjoying lunch in the United States with a friend who has traveled to Africa with me several times, I listened as he reminded me of one of his most vivid memories. He talked about the day we went to visit a village grandmother who had been ferociously attacked by a water buffalo four weeks before our arrival. The woman was sitting on a worn, faded green and yellow plaid rug that was placed over the dirt floor in her small dark hut. Although the temperature approached 100 degrees Fahrenheit that day, she was draped in a red wool blanket that was tattered at the edges. She seemed to be wearing it as protection from something. She was unable to leave her home, as the attack left her unable to walk. She was very hot and very dusty, and she looked at me with uncertainty.

Her granddaughter joined us, and the elderly woman seemed to relax a bit. As I sat beside her and told her about myself and my family, I asked if she would share with me what had happened. She said that she was sitting outside of her hut, guarding the small garden that she had planted to feed her family. The animals were as hungry as the people who lived in this village, and they foraged for food in the evening hours, so it was important to guard your crops from these predators. She did that by banging on pots with a thick wooden spoon to keep the animals at bay.

As night fell, the grandmother fell asleep. The metal pot and wooden spoon fell to the ground. She was abruptly and painfully awakened by an intruding water buffalo. I have seen these animals. They are very large, strong creatures with big horns. Their behavior is unpredictable, making them very dangerous to humans.

The woman said the water buffalo lifted her up and tossed her a distance. She broke her hip, knee, and ankle in the fall. Her right foot and ankle looked like they were fused into one large ball of skin and tissue. Her injured left arm hung loosely by her side. With no medical care available, she was forced to live her life propped up sitting in her hut.

I asked her about her pain level. She said that the pain was so constant and so strong but that it had now become just another part of her with which she has had to make peace. I asked if she would allow me to help her bathe and wash her hair using some hygiene supplies that I carried in my backpack. She agreed, and her granddaughter went off to fetch a large basin of water. I brushed her hair then we held hands until her granddaughter returned.

I helped her to bathe, her first full bath in some time. As I rinsed the shampoo from her hair, I could feel her relax even more. I applied a moisturizing balm to her deeply cracked lips and lotion to her very dry skin. She talked about her longing for what waits her in Heaven, but, as she said, "When God tells me that my work here is done." And just then, for the first time, she smiled such a radiant smile.

Once she was dressed in a new blue and yellow striped cotton house dress, two team members carried her outside. On the way out, she asked me how long she could keep the dress. "Always," I replied. She mustered a weak smile. As they moved to seat her under a shade tree, she asked that they allow her to sit in the full sunshine. They did so, and as she settled into the blankets that now surrounded her with support, she looked into the cloudless sky and closed her eyes. A single large tear escaped her right eye and gently rolled over the folds of her worn and beautiful face. She rested so serenely like that for several minutes. We provided food for the family, and with big hugs, and at her request, we left her there to enjoy the warmth of the sun on her face as she slowly sipped her tea and savored her crackers.

No wonder this memory stayed with my teammate. Can you imagine needing to sit up all night to protect your tiny garden? The garden that your children and grandchildren need to survive? Then to be tossed like a rag doll by a huge beast in the middle of the night? Then to have no access to a doctor or pain relief or a wheelchair for some mobility and independence?

I am so thankful for all that I learned from this lovely woman. She told me that when her work here is done, she prays that her path ahead will be much less painful. I hope that her prayers are answered.

Then there are the other large creatures, the baboons. These big, hairy monkeys are opportunists and are known to forage for food and to steal food from women and children. In one town center, the men described how a woman had just purchased a long loaf of fresh bread and was walking along the road to return to her home. A baboon quietly joined in step behind her, mimicking the way she walked. At an opportune time, the baboon then snatched the entire loaf of bread from the woman's arm, and ran off into the bush. The men said sightings like these are common.

Once, when our team traveled into the nearest city for project supplies, I spotted a baboon casually leaning against a tree, using a plastic spoon to eat leftover yogurt from a carelessly discarded plastic container. He seemed to be enjoying this. At the time, this seemed like an amusing tourist sight. Later I witnessed what fierce fighters these animals can be.

After spending the night in a local hospital watching over a teammate who had fallen ill from extreme dehydration, I returned to our place of lodging too late to depart for our project site with the rest of our team. A driver was available to take me, so we set off on the hour-long drive. On the outskirts of town, but at a distance from the road, I noticed a tall garbage dump occupying a vast open space. I saw what appeared to be two people fighting over something. As we drove closer to the dump, I was stunned to see that the fight was between a raggedly dressed man and a much larger baboon. They were each fiercely tugging at a loaf of discarded bread.

I looked at my driver to see if he noticed. He appeared to have not. So I asked, "Did you see that baboon fighting that poor man for some bread?" Without a glance towards the dump, he replied that this is a common occurrence, as animals and humans both try to feed themselves and their families from these dumps. With no trace of emotion, he added, "The baboon will win the fight. The baboon always wins. But the man will be rewarded in heaven for fighting to feed his starving family. It will come around in a circle back to him in the end."

I thought about that man for a long time, wondering if he ever found food, wondering what it is like to fight a baboon for an old stale loaf of bread that someone discarded in a garbage dump. My entire definition of "being hungry" had changed.

Hunger! Hunger!
(written by a boy, age 14)

Everywhere people cry because of you Hunger!
Who really created you?
You kill people, especially the poor.
The young ones cry because of Hunger.
Why do you kill people who never committed a crime?
Hunger does not discriminate,
It takes the young ones and the adults.
It is made worse by drought.
Hunger is dangerous, it leads to slow painful death.

Invasive Species

As I walked down a street in Africa looking for a painting to take home as a gift for someone who had donated to a project that I was collaboratively initiating in a nearby village, a dark green bus full of non-African men who appeared to be tourists pulled up alongside of the road. One man with an expensive-looking camera jumped out. He rushed straight towards a beautiful young mother and her even more beautiful young daughter who were walking down the road. Both were clothed in torn dresses with buttons missing and they wore no shoes. That mattered not as they were basking in the glow of their mother-daughter bond that day.

Without a word, this man roughly pushed the mother aside and began to take a series of close-up pictures of this now very frightened little girl. The mother was equally frightened and stunned. I ran over and asked what he was doing. He explained that he saw this little girl from the bus window and wanted to get a good picture of her because he thought that she would be so photogenic, something he could post on his social platform. It must have been the expression on my face, because he threw his hands in the air and said, "What?" What? That was the best he could do in that moment?

I talked to him about human dignity, protecting children, respecting this little girl's mother, his selfish actions. I asked him how he would feel if a stranger came to his country and did that to his wife and child? He replied, "But these are Africans." I am sure that I sighed a very loud sigh and rolled my eyes. I said that if he was going to take a picture like that, he first should ask and obtain permission and that he should be planning to use it to bring some relief to these good people, or at the very least, to raise awareness of their needs. I talked about how a camera could be a good weapon against poverty, disparities, and social injustices if used properly and respectfully.

He seemed to listen, and actually start to understand, but then he said, "Oh, right, I should have offered her, like, five dollars." Ugh!!! I suggested he just get back on the bus and keep moving – far, far away. I also suggested he ask this woman and child for forgiveness for his rudeness. He called me a very stupid woman and told me to mind my own business.

Just then the little girl said something in her tribal language. Several people on the tourist bus, who until this moment had been very quietly observing, began to laugh, then clap, when their local tour guide translated the girl's comment. I asked the mother what her daughter just said. She replied, "Why does this ugly man not know how to behave like a human?" Hearing that, begrudgingly and confused, the man got back on the bus, knowing he and his camera were unwelcome there.

The mother proudly said, "My little girl is smart." I said, "So is her mother." We both smiled, as she reached again for her daughter's hand, holding it a little more tightly now, as they continued on their journey.

As a volunteer, carefully consider how you use your camera. Ask yourself what is your intent in taking a picture and how you will use your pictures. Are you contributing to public misperceptions? Are you preserving dignity? Also ask yourself, "What would I do if someone asked me for money for taking his or her picture without permission?" That happens in remote villages and in certain tribes because you are an intruding stranger and they have no idea what you plan to do with their pictures or the pictures that you just snapped of their children. If you were back in your own community, would you take that same picture? Remember to be ethical, humble and respectful with your camera. Avoid what has been coined as "poverty porn," pictures taken to elicit an emotional response that may not fully represent the true overall circumstances. Consider always including pictures of your host community's strengths.

Decisions Made by the Heart
(written by a boy, age 15)

Think about it,
Do you think it's true that one decides to be rich or poor?
There is a choice to be made each time you get a hold of money.
Life is what you make it.
Just like boiling water which will either keep boiling and boil out,

Or with no flame, cools back to room temperature.
You decide on what to do or what to be by your heart.
Some vices are left out because we never discover
    their good side or are ignorant about them,
Or we have received too much of them.
But with every step you take, you learn a new skill,
To make a change in your life.
It's the decision from your heart
    to observe and absorb a change for its good,
Or to reject it for the bad it would cause.
Make good decisions.

Umbrella Bus

As a volunteer, you will encounter local traditions. One of my favorites is called *daima mbele*, Swahili for "always forward." I partnered with a nonprofit organization working on an African island and saw this phrase translated into truly meaningful acts of kindness. The experience was so heartwarming. The teenagers and young adults who are members of this nonprofit's clubs are always counseled to "Pay it forward." And that they did, with great pride and great caring for the people in their communities.

A chicken farm, a bicycle shop, and a nutrition program were all well-run initiatives led by local village youth under the guidance of this nonprofit organization. The Girls' Club also had several community service projects underway. They eagerly told me about the "Umbrella Bus" adventure. On a day of heavy monsoon rains, members from each of the clubs piled into an old bus and distributed umbrellas to those in need. They drove to a remote maternity center so that they could hand deliver these umbrellas to the new mothers and babies who were being discharged, often within hours of delivery, and both of whom would have been soaking wet in the relentless rain. What a great project!

I desired to experience this *daima mbele* first hand. The teenagers were excited, so off we went to purchase sixty large umbrellas. With the monsoon season in full swing, an umbrella was a precious commodity. During another day of drenching rains, we packed into their bus and headed off to distribute these large and colorful umbrellas to people struggling to walk through the streets in the nasty weather.

The rain was heavy and incessant. I had never seen such torrential downpours. Even the goats moved to shelter, hugging the wall of any building with an exterior overhang. The club members easily found people in need of an umbrella.

At first, several people were hesitant to take the umbrellas, fearing that if they did, they would be asked for money. The young people realized that they first needed to take the time to properly introduce themselves and explain *daima mbele*. With that, the sincerity in these teenagers shined through as they warmly engaged people stranded in the rain. The hesitation faded, and the umbrellas were quickly distributed with glee and excitement.

I watched an elderly man, using a wooden crutch, walk away happily carrying his new umbrella, then stop and look back to smile at the young man who had gifted him with this. I saw a woman whose foot was swollen and wrapped in plastic bags accept the umbrella while embracing the young girl who offered it to her. One of the youth noticed a petite young woman wearing no shoes, trying to navigate the slippery mud and the rain while carrying two children and a bag of fresh vegetables. He ran to her side, quickly shared his story, and then opened the umbrella over her, carried the bag of food, and led them all to nearby shelter. She rewarded him with a beautiful smile of thanks, as the children waved goodbye until he was out of their sight.

What a beautiful experience to see the young people here graciously receive assistance through the nonprofit organization that was helping them to move forward, and then so earnestly pay it forward to others in need. This group's goal to learn about social responsibility and sharing experiences to shape personal paradigms and relationships was met with flying colors. The jubilant "Umbrella Bus" will always remain a special memory in my heart, and a reminder to me to constantly find and offer my own *daima mbele* to others. If your path crosses this tradition of *daima mbele*, do not hesitate to jump on board for this heartwarming adventure.

The African Child
(written by a boy, age 14)

People say....
The African Child doesn't want more shirts.
They are ever dirty.
Sometimes they are street kids.
They are full of making crimes.
They are black in color.
That's why they commit crimes in the darkness,
Which leads to arrests by police,
Which causes hatred between parents and the police.
People say…
The African child is ever arrogant.
They are full of bad behaviors.
And they don't mind others.
Sometimes they care only for themselves.
And they don't want schooling,
Which leads to lack of employment.
People say…
The Africa child is shabby.
They don't want to be told the right way to follow.
They are ever creating enemies,
And destroying friendships,
Which leads to division of the African child.
Listen to your parents, think about others, go to school.
When people say these things…
Remember that they judge and do not even know us.
Remember that they are not correct about what they say.
Do NOT listen to what "people say".
We know that we are not that child.

Curious Questions

As your volunteer efforts in Africa grow, you will likely find more and more people asking seemingly personal questions. Be prepared with solid answers, and ones that do not convey defensiveness. Sometimes people are just curious. Sometimes they just have a false perception of life in African villages.

After a decade of volunteering, I noticed themes in the questions that I am asked, most often from people who have never traveled to Africa. Some people very mistakenly romanticize the volunteer work, with images of our teams rushing in to be the saviors of the poor. Sometimes they believe that when our teams wake up in the villages, the first things we see are lions, giraffes and elephants roaming the schoolyard. They often are a tad disappointed to learn that neither is true. They seem even more disappointed to learn that most mornings the animals roaming the schoolyard are chickens and goats, and one rooster which loudly crows just before the crack of dawn.

Being a married female volunteer, I am frequently asked, "How did you get your husband to let you travel there without him?" I suppress the urge to smile as I think about how preposterous my very supportive husband would find this question. When I am in Africa, my husband grows a scratchy beard on his usually clean-shaven face, and he uses that change in his physical appearance to elicit questions from people so that he has an opportunity to share my stories about Africa. Most often I respond to this question by explaining how supportive he is, ignoring any other connotations that question might hold.

I have seen similar personal questions posed to our young travelers such as, "How do your parents feel about you being in Africa instead of getting a job or going to college?" Use those as educational opportunities to share your passion about the volunteer work that draws you to Africa.

Another question that is frequently posed by people who inquire about the volunteer work that I do is, "I have heard that AIDS is everywhere there. Aren't you worried about catching it?" This is a valuable teaching moment and a question I always welcome. I ask the person if they know the infection rate in their own United States community. Some are enlightened. Some become very uncomfortable with the thought that this virus might be found in their own community. This is a good opportunity to educate people about this virus and how it is transmitted. I ask people how they became misinformed that every person in Africa has HIV/AIDS. Then I share the facts about the large and often quite effective campaigns to fight HIV/AIDS and the struggles to sustain treatment options in some African countries.

Often I am asked if took pictures on my trip. Often the person asking the question is disappointed that my pictures did not include more of the exotic animals or famous landmarks. The more I traveled to volunteer in Africa, the less I used my camera. That change allowed me to focus on what was most important – the people. Think very introspectively about why you want to volunteer in Africa. Are you looking to learn and strengthen your global awareness and problem-solving skills? Are you hoping to add bulk to your resume? Is your focus on the long-term needs defined by your African host community? Then ask yourself this question, "Would I go if I had to leave my camera (or phone) at home?"

Look at life in Africa through the lens of someone who lives there. I met a brilliant photographer who lives in East Africa. She has a magnificent way of capturing the true heart of Africa and its people. Through her photographs, I grew more and more able to readily see this beauty myself. If you are blessed to meet someone like her, forge a strong connection you can maintain over time. She will continue to enrich you in many ways.

Many people have said, "I could never do what you do. I mean, you must really have thick skin to deal with all of that stuff, right?" You don't need to do what I do. This is my calling. But you might be able to help just one person somewhere with something small. That would be equally as important. As for thick skin, I really do not have that. I do try to always have a warm heart. Some experiences still knock the wind out of me, as they should. That is how I learn. As a volunteer you will have the wind knocked out of you on some days. Just breathe in through your nose and out through your mouth until that eases. Then analyze how you can use that experience for good purposes going forward.

One of the most common questions addressed to me is, "There are so many people in our own country who need help. Why do you feel the need to work in Africa instead of here? Don't you think charity begins at home?" The first few times I replied to this charity begins at home question, I did not realize the questioner was looking for a one-sided debate. I took the time to explain the volunteer work I do in the United States in addition to the volunteer work I do in Africa. Often that response was met with strong pushback, again emphasizing the belief that one should focus volunteer efforts solely in his or her homeland. Those conversations left me very unsettled and feeling like I was being negatively judged for reasons I did not understand.

But then one day I read this quote attributed to Mahatma Gandhi: "I have learnt through bitter experience the one supreme lesson to conserve my anger, and as heat conserved is transmuted into energy, even so our anger controlled can be transmuted into a power which can move the world."

One quote about harnessing anger helped me to change my approach to the charity begins at home question. Now I respond, "You are right that the need for help is everywhere, and yes, so much so here in our own country. I am always looking for opportunities to help. So tell me about what you are doing to help here at home in the US, and maybe we can join forces." The answer is always the same, "I, umm, I don't do anything like that, I mean, well, I haven't given it any thought. I don't really get involved like that." I usually let them off the hook at that point by nicely saying "OK, well when you do reach out to help someone at home, give me a call and I would be more than willing to see how I can assist your efforts too." Yes, conserving my anger and turning it into energy can move the world. As an international volunteer, you too might need to redirect your actions when someone is fueling your fire.

Responsibility, Love and Life
(written by a boy, age 15)

When you say sorry, say it with gravity,
Be sorry for yourself as well.
When you are loved, don't take it for granted,

Take responsibility as well as loving back.
When you are forgiven, forget your past traits,
Learn to change.
If you doubt this, then ask me.
Have you ever paid a visit to nature in a city of loneliness?
Door slammed in your face?
No money to pay the rent?
The whole world turned against you?
Living under heavy rain and too much coldness?
Has home ever lost its meaning?
And only Death can accept you?
But right before you jump off the bridge to drown,
A voice calls you for a new life and a new hope.
What do you do?
Whatever you think, it's within your own hands.

Why Go?

People ask me why I do not just send funds instead of spending so much money on airfare to travel to Africa. I tell them I have learned that relationship is the currency of Africa. Teams come and go, but people in these villages want to know they matter to someone in this world and that their stories will be told. They want to know they are not just a volunteer's "mission project." They want to learn your names and for visitors to learn their names. They want to shake hands or exchange a warm hug with someone who cares that they exist. I have learned so much more on many levels from those people than I have ever taught them. They have gifted me in ways I could never repay. In one village, I was bestowed an African tribal name of Ngirozi Y orugare, meaning "Angel of Peace"; however, these people are the angels who educate me and fill me with peace. Being with them is such a privilege. Being there with them allows me to then be their witness, to be their voice, and to raise awareness of what I experience with them. That is why I spend my own personal money on airfare and lodging in Africa rather than just sending money. Relationships. It is money well spent.

Once your eyes are opened to the deepest depths of the problems in the world, once you immerse yourself in this culture and witness the trials yourself, your heart will not allow you to ever go back to ignoring those problems and the people who suffer. And you find that it gets in your blood, and you become aware that you would not want to change your new gift of insight or the desire to help. You will witness incredible physical and mental strength and spirit, and unshakeable faith. In these villages, mind, body, and spirit are in sync. You will absorb more than you could ever give. If you are called, go. In going and giving, you will be nourished in a unique and incredible way. The self-transformation is progressive, unfolding with each new journey.

On one trip, while volunteering at a remote village school, my teammate and I pulled colored sidewalk chalk out of our supply bag. We were not facing each other, but we drew exactly the same thing on the school's cement walkway at exactly the same time – big matching hearts. One of the children then drew a heart to connect these two. We looked at each other with big smiles, for this is what this work is all about – learning more and more how very much alike we are: identical hearts working side by side with no agenda other than to try to relieve pain and suffering, to learn and grow by this giving, and to share a little peace on Earth.

The hardest part of any trip is not the risk of malaria or cholera or other medical conditions. It is not the potential attack by a black scorpion or the Nairobi fly. It is not the heat and humidity. It is not well-founded concerns about contaminated drinking water or eating foods that may result in severe abdominal distress. It is not the thirty or more hours of travel each way, with the likelihood of flight delays that further extend that travel time. It is not the extensive planning and packing and fundraising prior to the trip itself. It is not the lack of running water or electricity or bathrooms. It is not the occasional minor earthquake that moves your bed a bit at night. It is not getting used to the big lizards scampering over the walls of your sleeping quarters. It is not sleeping in a room with twelve other people who you may or may not have ever met before, some of them snoring at night. It is not having no idea what to do when a snorting 120-pound warthog is walking right towards you. It is not having trouble peeing in an outdoor pit latrine because there is a donkey poking its head inside to see what you are doing. It is not having a bat fly through your room at night and then get stuck in your long hair, while you and the bat look at each other as you both loudly shriek.

The hardest part always is leaving; leaving such wonderful new and old friends who you grow to love through their teachings, knowing that there is still so much to learn and so much more work to do, with so many who need help. The final hugs are not goodbyes. They are promises that they will be remembered and that their stories will be told.

<u>The Beautiful Angel</u>
(written by a boy, age 15)

The girl I first loved, beautiful like an angel,
Brighter than the sunset,
Joyous like a puppy,
Happy as a king,
She is really so beautiful.
She is shinier than the sun, humble and patient.
I will never leave this beautiful one.
She is smarter than you can predict,
She is the angel in this world.
She moves smartly, gently, happily,
She won the beauty race of the year,
Some do fear her because she is smoother,
    more intelligent than them,
She is really amazing.
I will stay long with my Only One,
No better is accepted.
So listen all - Stay Away!

Why Take Dolls or Other Frivolous Things?

After sending forty-foot shipping containers to Africa more than once, I finally realized that those material shipments are far from what this work is all about for me. While they certainly and often may have their place in projects, that is not where I personally now want to invest my time and efforts. Nor do I see materialism as the answer to serious problems. That often creates worse problems, like theft and begging, which may not have formerly existed. I do, however, continue to take small duffle bags full of purposeful and requested supplies for schools and clinics and to assist with materials needed for the specific projects to which I am directly contributing.

I learned to instead give of myself, more than anything else. I learned not to bring things no one had asked for. I learned to hug more and to allow my lap to be a seat for any child who needed a comforting hug, instead of space for a piece of luggage. I learned to quiet my voice, soften my ego, and stop talking so that I truly listen more. Perhaps it is no coincidence that the words "listen" and "silent" have the exact same letters.

Sometimes, though, I carry items that people question. Why would you use your precious luggage space for that? Couldn't they use something better than that?

I do think about this very carefully as I pack for each trip. Sometimes a donation is offered that on the surface seems frivolous and self-serving. But at times, and in conjunction with discussions and agreement with our African project managers, that donation may actually serve a unique need.

One example is the blessing of some donated dolls that made a difference and were worth every inch of that duffle bag's space. A wonderful nonprofit organization makes soft cloth dolls, boy and girl models, out of colorful high-quality material. All of the dolls have big smiling faces and are quite diverse in skin color and attire. Each is tagged with a name. All are outfitted with clothes, a knitted blanket and a carrying tote. They are simply beautiful, and are meant to bring faith, love, joy, hope, and comfort to children worldwide at times of special need.

With the teacher's prior consent, we distributed these dolls to the kindergarten class at a village school. That is when I witnessed the purest joy I have ever seen in a child. These little ones were ecstatic and barely able to sit down in their seats. Smiles were unending and these little faces just glowed. They hugged their babies so tightly and loved learning their names. Then they wrapped them in their blankets and never once put them down. I thought they would burst from the happiness of owning their very first personal possession of any kind. As I was leaving the school for the day, one little girl was taking the underwear off her doll. I thought it was because the girl herself had no underwear to wear. But when I asked her, she whispered, "We both have to go pee!" And she and her doll ran off to do so. Watching her run as she toted her little Suzanna kept me smiling for a long time.

The next day, the mothers of these students came to the school to tell us that their children fell asleep with their dolls in their arms, and that they have never had such good sleep – no nightmares, no waking up in fear, no worries, just peaceful sleep. The children brought the dolls to school that next day, sat them on their laps and instructed them to listen so that they could all learn their letters and numbers. The teacher was so happy to have such positive, focused energy in her classroom. She said that she had never seen the children so concentrated on their schoolwork as when they channeled their studies through the dolls. She also observed that the most reserved and quiet students seemed to be more willing to openly participate in class. It is difficult to describe in words how the dolls seemed to transform these children, for in the comfort of caring for the dolls, the children were also finding comfort within themselves. The dolls had become a new learning medium for these children.

When we gave some of the dolls to a group of orphans, they called us into their bedrooms when it grew dark outside to show us the dolls all tucked into their beds under their little blankets. The dolls were smiling as they always do – and so were the children! I noticed all of the dolls' dresses were neatly laid out at the bottom of the beds. I asked why they removed their dresses and the girls replied, "Oh, she must rest now, then get up and look smart tomorrow for school lessons!" There, when you tell someone that they look very nice, you say, "You look smart today." It is quite a compliment. So these little ones wanted their dolls to look "smart" in the morning, freshly clothed in unwrinkled dresses.

The next day, the orphans' caretaker shared that for the first time, every child slept soundly throughout the night, knowing that the dolls were snuggly tucked into bed with them. She also observed the children talking to each other about difficult thoughts and feelings, but doing so by speaking through the dolls, using them as props. The caretaker thought this was very good emotional therapy for the children.

We delivered the remaining dolls to a women's prison, where I found myself choking back tears. Some of the mothers who are incarcerated there have no one to care for their children, so the children reside at the prison as well. Each toddler lovingly hugged his or her doll and it was a beautiful sight to see the smiles on these young children who lived a harsh, confined life.

Each infant also received a doll for when he or she was old enough to play with it. These dolls were the ones which had such an impact. The mothers who have no children or whose children live with relatives until they are released from prison picked up these dolls and cradled them as if they were real children. They rocked them in their arms and cuddled them against their shoulders, lovingly patting them on the back.

At one point during my time there, I did not realize that some of the women were holding a doll instead of a real child. They gently wrapped their blankets around them and when they all danced and sang for us, these women continued to cradle these dolls as if they were their real babies. I saw tears in some of the women's eyes as they gazed tenderly upon the smiling faces of these dolls. Earlier in the day, one of the women shared that her daughter lives with relatives until her release from prison, and she has not seen her in a long while. As I left for the day, this woman whispered, "Thank you, I feel my child so closely with me today. Am blessed."

Use your luggage space wisely. Experience will lead you to a better understanding of the difference between supplies that make you as the receiver feel good and supplies that are best for the people awaiting your arrival. Work with the locals, the village elders, and the nonprofit leaders with whom you are traveling to assess the actual needs and to obtain agreement on that. Determine what supplies you can purchase at your project site to support the local economy there. Whatever you do bring, never hand out supplies indiscriminately. This is most important so as to not contribute to a begging culture, especially with the children.

Mother
(written by a girl, age 14)

Oh Mother, Mother,
What a wonderful mother you are!
What a caring mother you are,
You are so loved.
Oh Mother,
You are the light of my life.
Oh how I wish to stay with you always Mother,
My sweet Mother.
Oh Mother, Mother,
You managed to carry me for 9 months in your womb,
You were ever there in times of trouble,
What a loving mother you are.
Oh Mother, Mother,
Thank you for being my mother.

Aha! Moments and Short Stories

Each day volunteering in an African village is a new learning experience. The spirituality and fellowship that I experienced there continue to fill my heart with joy. Keep a journal to record each day's events and to track your daily thoughts and observations. The following pearls of wisdom are from my own experiences.

The Center of Attention

One of our team members, a spirited young college student, clearly loved spending time with the African children. When we went to visit the local elementary school, she quickly rounded up sixteen of the students, both boys and girls, and ushered them into a nearby field. The children sat down, forming a circle, and she plopped herself in the middle of that circle, facing eight boys. Then with great confidence, she proceeded to ask, "So, OK, who wants to be the first one to ask me a question?" One lovely young girl raised her hand, and our college girl smiled and assuredly said, "OK, so what it is that I can teach you today?" The girl said, "I was wondering if you could tell us if Rhianna and Chris Brown ever got back together?" Our college girl was speechless, absolutely speechless, likely for the first time in her life. She looked up at me with a bewildered look on her face. I softly said, "Go ahead and answer her question." She regained her composure and her voice, and did just that.

They continued to have a great discussion, as our college girl learned to also ask her audience questions herself. Later that day, we shared a good laugh about her reaction to that first question and how she thought that she was holding court, not realizing that she was actually part of the circle instead of the special centerpiece. "We are all the same," I said. She replied, "And I had to come halfway around the world to learn that from students half my age!" Be aware and don't make yourself the center of attention.

Unity

As you develop relationships with people in Africa, at some point, they may travel to the United States as your guest. They will likely learn many things in your country, but they will also continue to be great teachers from their country. One year, we were honored to have our project manager from Africa visit the United States as the guest speaker at our not-for-profit organization's annual dinner. At one point in his talk, he emphasized how we all could, if we choose, be part of the worldwide fight against famine, poverty, child trafficking, and oppression. He held up his right hand with his fingers spread far apart. He noted how the fingers on his hand were not equal to each other. Some were short, some were longer. And that each had a different but equally important role to play on his hand. Then he emphatically clenched those fingers into a tight fist and raised that fist into the air, representing unity of the unequal parts. He said that together, with our differences tightly bound in unity, we can make a real and meaningful difference. He has seen so much inequality in his life, so much sorrow. Yet he never stops fighting for human rights and dignity. I applauded his raised fist of unity that fights against oppression, and so did the entire room of people who rose to their feet in full support.

Thanksgiving

As we waited to test the newly installed solar panel which would provide the first ever evening light in a village, four women approached. They were quite elderly, wore no shoes, and their feet and hands appeared to be swollen. Their lips were parched, yet their eyes were shining. On this very hot day, they had slowly walked several miles from their church on the hill overlooking our project site. Their leader said they were the Prayer and Thanksgiving group.

The women had been praying for five years that assistance be sent to the women and children of this village, and now that it had come, they were there to sing songs of thanksgiving. They sang loudly, and joyously, in appreciation for blessings delivered. One woman clasped her worn hands in prayer. One woman kept her eyes closed, with her face lifted towards the sky. One woman held her hand over her heart as she sang. One woman who appeared to be the oldest of the four grasped my hand ever so tightly and squeezed with a strength that I had not expected.

They truly had walked that far just to sing for us. Their voices raised in song sounded angelic, and I found this to be a very emotional moment. They hugged our team members and comforted us, instead of the other way around. Then, in great peace, and with their song continuing to fill the air, they turned to start their long journey home before dark, singing the song "Amazing Grace." Always take the time to watch and learn from the elderly in the village. What amazing grace they possess. Always respect that.

Time with Young People

A twelve-year-old girl who lived in a remote village told me that she wants to go to New York with me. I asked her what she would do in New York. Without hesitation, she replied, "Preach the Word of God – and eat pizza. Do you have pizza in New York?" I asked her if she had ever tasted pizza. She had not, but she was sure that if she preached the Word of God that someone would feed her with pizza! She explained that she had heard that this is what Americans do to make visitors happy: they serve them pizza. Maybe she has a point. Pizza does make me happy.

Later that day, our team prepared dinner to be served to our team and the adults and children at our project site. Several team members helped our host peel and dice many pounds of potatoes, carrots, tomatoes, other vegetables, and fresh fruit. Our host was a fabulous cook and she was excited to prepare a special meal for everyone. She did all of the cooking on small outdoor charcoal stoves. That alone was just amazing. We were served chicken, goat, boiled potatoes, carrots, cole slaw, rice, brown beans, spaghetti noodles, salads, matoke (a cooking/green banana), and other delights. The children most often eat posho (cornmeal) and beans, so they were thrilled to have such a variety of offerings. They eagerly filled their plates with modest portions and moved to sit outside to savor their dinner. I joined them for some great discussion and good laughter.

When I invited the children for a second helping, the oldest boy, who was about eight or nine years of age, immediately stood up, stopped everyone and asked me, "Has everyone else eaten already?" They had not yet, as some guests were just arriving, but I assured him that we had plenty of food. He firmly said, "We will wait until all have eaten." When the children did return for seconds, they formed a straight, single-file line and he made sure that the thin little children were up front. Then he helped each of them with their plates. He was last in line, and although he was perhaps the oldest, he was just a child himself.

Spend as much time as possible with young children and teenagers. Do not be surprised if many of them tell you that they hope to become a doctor one day. Ask them why, and you will gain deeper insight to their lives. Remember that some of them may not know their actual age or birthdate, so be sensitive to that.

Full Hearts

I distributed a connect-the-dots activity to the children in an orphanage. As they drew a line from letters A to B to C, they realized they were making a big heart. I then asked them to take this drawing, and using crayons, depict what was in their own hearts on that day. One boy drew black clouds with large rain drops falling from them. His picture matched the heavy monsoon rains that we watched from the window. A girl drew bright red and yellow flowers, which she said would blossom after the rains. One girl drew a picture of a little girl, a little boy, a mother, a father, and a cat. I asked if this was someone who she knew or some part of her family. She solemnly replied, "No, Teacher. I have no family in my life. But this is the family that I hope that I will have one day. Even the cat." I hoped that this little one's wish one day becomes her reality.

Consider how you would respond to a story from a child with no parent, and often no other family.

Baby Joy

We met with some village women to share birthing kits we had assembled. Mothers here could not afford these very basic supplies (each kit included a bar of soap, one pair of gloves, plastic sheeting, gauze squares, cotton string, a razor blade, a receiving blanket, a plastic bag, and a baby cap), nor could they afford thirty-five dollars for a formal Mama Kit sold in the nearest town. Glorious cheers erupted when we showed them the contents of these kits. The pregnant mothers then came forward to receive their kits. One young pregnant woman excitedly said, "I will no longer be in such great anxiety about my baby coming through birth, no matter what comes to be."

Later that day, one young woman quietly approached me for a packet, as she preferred some privacy. As she accepted this kit, she bowed and then knelt down. I protested and told her that we are all in this together, women helping women, learning from each other. She said, "I accept this assistance with great appreciation and humbleness. I have lost two children in birthing. I had no help. I had much pain. I prayed for a baby again but only if this one could be born and be mine. But I had little hope for this blessing to be true. Yesterday I learned that I am again with child. No one else knows. Today I am assured that my prayers were answered." We hugged each other tightly.

Be prepared for these unexpected moments of shared trust and joy. Maintain the trust that is placed in you. Appreciate the blessing of the moment.

Hand Sandals

As our van transported us to our project site one day, we came to a sudden halt due to excessive vehicle and pedestrian foot traffic congestion. I could hear the repeated sound of "flip flop, flip flop." I looked out the bus window and I saw a man crawling on the ground, with thin, red flip-flop sandals on the palms of his hands to help propel him forward. His body twisted in all sorts of contortions as he slowly dragged his torso around. He navigated through the crowds with difficulty, yet his unreadable expression never changed. His face was coated with the dirt from the street. Someone said he was affected by polio.

To everyone else outside of my window, this appeared to be a normal experience in this town. But for me, I was reminded of how this is not a normal experience in my own hometown. I did not know anyone afflicted by polio. I never knew old, faded sandals could be used as mobility aids like this. As the traffic gridlock began to dissipate, our van moved forward. The flip-flop sounds began to fade. I desperately wished I knew how to help. I offered up prayers for this man and others like him, feeling like it was not enough, that I needed to do more. I continue to become more acutely aware of how much more I need to learn about life outside of my own small circle. This volunteer work has helped me to expand my circle. Continue to widen your own circle of knowledge.

T is for Teacher

On one trip, our team brought large white squares with letters of the alphabet and colorful pictures depicting those letters for the new preschool that we had built. After these had been taped to the wall, and the children practiced their letters for several days, the teacher invited us to see how their learning had progressed. A very confident little girl took the teacher's long pointer and began, saying, "A is for apple. B is for boy. C is for cat." She continued through the alphabet to letter Z for zebra. We praised her display of quick learning and she beamed. Later I asked her about letter Y, which she said is for yacht. I asked her if she knew what a yacht is. She shook her head and replied, "No, not at all. But I do know that it starts with the letter Y and that is has something to do with the big boat on this picture."That was a good answer! But maybe next time, we should consider bringing a teaching tool to which the children could better relate.

Privacy Please

Before departing for one African trip, I was asked to add journals to the orphanage's requested supply list. The specific ask was for journals with locks and keys. I had already planned to facilitate a poetry class with the children living at this orphanage, as on previous trips to Africa, I had found the poetry-writing class to be a valuable assist in learning about the children's inner world.

When I met with the children at the orphanage, we spent an hour studying different types of poetic styles and reading works from well-known poets. The children then opened their journals and for the next hour, they silently and diligently captured their own original poems and thoughts on the paper. They did ask to share some of their writings, and this provided great insight into their request for journals with locks to which they were the keeper of the keys. Their notations were filled with their deepest fears and sadness, feelings of loss, and drivers of hope for the future.

I asked the children specifically why they requested journals with locks as their number one need. The oldest girl explained the doors to their rooms at the orphanage are never locked, and must always remain open, so there is no privacy. Anyone may enter a room and peruse your assigned space. The children wanted to be able to document their most inner thoughts, and for that to be a private matter for their eyes only. Journals with locks provided them with the comfort and peace of mind that their personal thoughts remained personal. A young adult woman who was assisting me with this class explained she had grown up in this orphanage and during that time, a volunteer provided her with a journal with a lock and key to capture her thoughts. She shared she found great comfort in that, both then and reflecting on her writings now.

As I left the classroom, I turned to inhale the beauty of these children one last time. They continued to earnestly and intently write in their journals. The room was filled with peaceful silence.

Sometimes you will be asked for a donated supply that seemingly has no direct tie to the projects in which you will be involved. If you encounter that, just ask the children. They are very willing teachers.

Puzzled

Have you ever watched a child put together a jigsaw puzzle for the first time? Children in a village I was visiting had never seen a puzzle before. When I distributed several of them, the children had a difficult time understanding what to do with them. At first, they spent time trying to force mismatched pieces together. But after we slowly worked through one as a group, the children gleefully began to use their cognitive skills and were soon able to assemble the pieces to create the picture. Watching them make the connection that the picture on the box was the same as what they just assembled was such a delightful gift. Once they conquered understanding the relationship between the puzzle pieces and the final picture, they ran to different people on our team to demonstrate how to do the puzzles. They were beaming with pride over their finished masterpieces and it was a joy watching them develop those skills.

The puzzles were just ninety-nine cents each. It was a priceless return on investment and definitely worth the luggage space.

Hair Flair

Many of the very young African schoolgirls I have met wear their hair very short, cropped close to their heads. These girls were fascinated by my long, straight hair, especially if they have never seen hair that extends below one's shoulders. They would braid it into all kinds of patterns, laughing and talking as they did so. Frequently I ended up looking quite silly, with braids protruding in all directions. They made comparisons to their very short, cropped hair. Often I am asked, "Is this your real hair?" "It is," I reply (but perhaps not always my real hair color). They ask, "Where did all of this hair come from?" Or sometimes, they say, "How does your brain grow that hair out of your head?"

Be prepared to have your long hair braided into all kinds of funky hair styles, and especially so if you are a male with a head full of hair. Enjoy the laughter and good-natured fun in these messy-hair-don't-care moments. This bonding is what makes for precious memories.

Building Community Strength

The young girls made their third trip to the well on another very hot day. They looked tired as they reached up high in the air to pull down the heavy metal arm of the well. A spray of water gushed forth with each laborious pull of the handle. I noticed several young, healthy-looking teenage boys sitting nearby just watching these young girls struggle with this chore. Pumping water, like most daily chores, was a job for the village girls, not the boys. I approached the well and asked if I too could help with this manual pumping. The girls graciously welcomed me. When I reached up high and pulled down on the handle, I was surprised by how very heavy it actually was. I gained immediate respect for the strength of these girls.

Seeing the difficulty that I was having with the weight of the well's pumping arm, an adorable six-year-old boy came to my rescue. "Teacher," he said, "Let me be of help to you." I thanked him and lifted him above my head so that he could grasp the arm of the pump with his little hands. All of the girls helped him to pull the lever down and up several times, producing gushes of water. This little one was beaming and he tried to make a muscle with his bicep to demonstrate his strength. "My, you are so strong," I said and I approvingly patted him on the back.

The watching teens noticed. "We are strong too," the tallest one said. "Well, I cannot judge without seeing that for myself," I replied. All six of the boys got up from their perches and began to quickly fill the girls' water jugs. The girls were surprised! Soon they realized what had just happened and I saw them exchange smiles. I admit that I felt a little badly about tricking these boys into helping the girls with their labor. But here they were, joining in with the work to be done rather than just ogling from the sidelines. As more and more of the water jugs were filled, the boys and girls began to interact, work together, and talk to each other. Their laughter filled the air.

The tallest boy then asked if I now thought that he too was strong. I replied, "Yes, of course. I see that. But if you are here tomorrow, I would need to see if this is something you could do again. That would demonstrate true strength." He looked to his friends and firmly said, "We will be here."

The girls were thrilled to have the help. This would make their burden lighter and take much less time. The rest of the week I watched as these boys arrived at the well to help pump the water. They seemed to be enjoying the task and proud of contributing to this work. I told them all how proud I was of them for their strength in working together like this.

Find ways to work in unison within your own volunteer team and community in which you are serving. Set the example.

Should I Stay or Should I Go?

As I headed to the village school one day to teach a literature class, I heard two girls yelling loudly. Everyone in the village stopped in their tracks. In this village, you never heard anyone raise his or her voice, ever, for any reason. This was a place where harmony was taught and expected. In less than two minutes, members of the village elder committee, four men and one woman, appeared. They motioned for the two young girls to sit before them. The girls obediently ended their argument and dropped to take a seat in the sand. The elder woman sternly chastised them for causing this disturbance, firmly reminding them that while the village culture allows for disagreements, those differences are not permitted to rise to the level of shouting at each other and creating disruption in the peaceful atmosphere. She asked, "What matter of great significance led to this violence?"

One of the girls lowered her eyes and softly said, "We are in disagreement about a boy who said he likes me but she says he likes her." I looked up and saw a handsome young boy anxiously watching from the wings. The elder woman sternly said, "In our community, we may disagree, but we do so in peaceful resolution. We do not shout. We do not raise our hands as if to strike. We discipline our actions. And we act with respect to all living things. You will be given two minutes to discuss between yourselves what happened. Then you will tell us your decision. Your choice is a permanent, peaceful resolution that you both find and agree upon the terms, or you must immediately leave our community to never return." She spoke very seriously.

The girls teared up and earnestly huddled in discussion. Soon they announced they were ready to speak. They joined hands, as one girl softly and respectfully said, "We have reached our decision. We will remain good friends. We will support each other and our entire community. We will always find peaceful ways to end our problems. For this particular situation, neither she nor I will be with this boy again. We apologize to you, our teachers, and our families and all of those who live here for our behaviors. We commit that we have learned." The elder woman suppressed a smile as she congratulated them on making a wise decision. As she watched the girls run off, still hand in hand, her face broke into a wide grin. And the boy in the background dejectedly walked away.

What a lesson in peaceful resolution! What a delightful learning experience for me!

Healthy Competition

During a day of adult education in an African village, our team taught a class on nutrition, using local produce and the color wheel to explain how brightly colored fruits and vegetables help us to fight disease and stay healthy. As part of that class, women were able to make their own pot holders. In previous trips, our team observed that cooking was done with charcoal over an open fire, so painful burns to one's hands were common. The women quickly learned how to use the looms and flame-resistant cloth loops, and the potholders began to take shape.

Two of the women suddenly realized they were working at an equal pace, and one of them would likely be the first to complete a potholder. The race was on, as these two women and a few others secretly upped their weaving speeds. Upon being the first one to complete her project, one of the competing women popped the pot holder off the loom, jumped up in excitement, held her product high in the air, and proudly displayed it to all who were present. In turn, we all cheered and applauded her accomplishment.

Then she turned to me and said, "Now, what IS this thing and what do I do with it?" That was not the question that I had anticipated, but I found myself good-naturedly laughing, not at her but at myself. Apparently I had not clearly explained to the women what they were making. I just told them how to make it. What was equally amusing is that the women all got caught up in the weaving process, wanting to be the first ones done to show their beautiful creations to the surrounding onlookers, and our team was caught up in that as well. One of our team members said, "I am just like her, racing like a chicken to get something done fast and first." We all laughed as we continued to bond as women. Then we took the time to explain what a potholder is and how it is used. The women were very happy to have something that would help to minimize burns from the open cooking fires.

Be sure that your projects have meaning and relevance to the area in which you are introducing them. Ask the villagers what they need, rather than assuming what you think they need. If you bring something new, take the time to explain what it is and what it does before you initiate the project. These small gatherings can be huge bonding experiences between you and the local people.

Commanding Attention

One day, I walked into a long rectangular cement classroom to teach and found myself looking at almost 150 children. They were all loudly talking and laughing with each other and had not noticed that the school's headmaster and I had arrived. I looked at the school headmaster with concern and said, "I don't think I can teach 150 students at one time." He assured me I could and went on to demonstrate how to command the class's attention. At the loud, strong claps of his hands, the children immediately ceased talking and turned their full attention to him.

He explained that the pattern of the clap was most important. Clap, clap, then a rapid series of clap, clap, clap. With the last clap, he slid his right hand over and beyond the palm of his stationary left hand, aiming it towards the students. I learned that this was the teacher's way of saying, "Attention, please," with the palm slide demonstrating that the teacher is sending his attention to the students. The students then returned that same clapping pattern and sliding of the palms toward the teacher, signifying the children were returning that attention back to the teacher. I started the lesson and had no problem being heard. And the students were paying attention throughout the entire lesson. What a great concept, this sending of respect and returning it in kind.

When teaching, find whatever works best for you and your class. African village classes are often quite large and very crowded. Sometimes children are sitting closely together on the floor due to the lack of desks. If you plan to use the blackboard, you may need to provide your own chalk as the school's supply may have been depleted. The same is true for paper, pencils, or other supplies. Remember to ask an experienced village schoolteacher for advice about any uncertainties you experience. Garnering attention can be as easy as a few short claps.

Go Eat Worms

During your travels, you may find opportunities to sample a local food that is unfamiliar to you. In one country, the town's tourist restaurant offered what they called an "African delicacy," the mopane worm. If you consumed one of the crunchy critters, you received a certificate of recognition of your accomplishment. The restaurant's chef explained that mopane worms are fried, and taste like dried, crunchy potato chips. The mopane worm is actually not a worm, but the caterpillar of a moth. It does look like a large caterpillar. He further enticed our team by saying the worms have high levels of iron, calcium, and protein.

I am not an adventurous eater at home or abroad. So when two members took the challenge and I watched them immediately flush the worms down with large amounts of water, I passed on the offer to earn that certificate. I felt the same about the plate of warthog. But some of our team members embraced these delicacies and thoroughly enjoyed the opportunity to try new foods. While eating something that has the insides squeezed out of it then fried until it is crispy and charcoal-grayish looking does not appeal to me, it may appeal to you.

One time I was offered, and declined, handfuls of protein-rich nsenene (bush crickets or grasshoppers), a special treat during the rainy season. Some of our team members thoroughly enjoyed these crunchy critters. I have tried rolex, which I originally thought was an offer to purchase an expensive watch. But this "rolled eggs," an egg omelet with vegetables rolled into a chapati (flatbread), was quite good.

The locals love when visitors embrace the food culture. And if you take the plunge, you too just might have a beautiful certificate of recognition to take home as a souvenir.

Rendered Defenseless, Not Dead

In an earlier story, I mentioned a pesky scorpion which parked itself outside of my sleeping quarters. This was the first, but not the last, scorpion that I encountered. So I did what many new volunteers do in that situation, I wildly screamed, "There is a scorpion by my shoes!" The hotel security guard calmly walked over and with one swift motion, lopped off the scorpion's tail. I watched it scamper away into the grass. I must have looked confused, for the guard said, "There is no need for it to die, just to have its weapon removed." That statement remains a memorable one for me.

On our arrival at this place of lodging, we were instructed to wear closed-toed shoes while walking through the grass in the gated compound. We were also told to shake out our shoes before we inserted our feet into them each morning. If your host advises you to use caution in order to avoid the painful sting of a scorpion, heed that advice.

Boy, oh Boy!

In rural villages I have visited, the schoolchildren all have very closely cropped hair. Clothing is also not a gender identifier. Never assume that a village child wearing a dress or skirt is a girl. Often a boy is clothed in his older sister's hand-me-down clothes, for that is all there is for him to wear. I made this mistake only once early on in my travels, and it was once too often. After spending thirty minutes talking to two of the young village children who were on their way to the well, I bid them farewell so that I could continue to my mission to visit people living in the most remote parts of this village. I waved goodbye and said, "Have a good afternoon, girls!" Their faces immediately fell, and their smiles vanished. One of the boys respectfully admonished me, saying, "Mama, we are BOYS!!" I tried to cover my mistake, but from then on, I was cautious to verify gender before assigning it to any child.

Quenching Your Thirst

Safe drinking water is of key importance when you are traveling to many remote international destinations. Some travelers use water filtration bottles and devices. Some use chemical water treatments. Some look for bottled water in sealed, tamper-proof plastic containers. Plastic water bottles may have been refilled with water that is unsafe for a nonresident to drink, resulting in unpleasant conditions such as traveler's diarrhea. If the bottle cap is too easy to remove, or if it seems like it was glued on instead of making a cracking noise upon opening, be wary of consuming the contents.

The same applies to the plastic wrappers over the cap. If the wrapper seems loose and the cap is also loose, that bottle may have been opened at least one other time. Use bottled or other safe water to brush your teeth and to rinse your toothbrush, something that many first-time travelers forget to consider. Boiled water used to make tea, coffee, and juice most often is safe to drink.

On several trips, volunteers on our team drank water from the village wells. Most often their purpose in doing so was to avoid the trek to our team's van to retrieve a bottle of safe drinking water. In that moment, in the middle of a work project or playing soccer in the field with the children on a very hot day, they convinced themselves that the very clear water flowing from the well would be OK to drink just that once. That never turned out to be a good long-term choice and resulted in sleepless nights for those team members. If I am leading a team, I carry saltine crackers and over-the-counter diarrheal medication with me should anyone have a lapse of good judgment like this. If symptoms persist or increase in severity, a practitioner likely should be consulted.

Are You Covered?

Regarding what to wear – go with conservative clothes. Check the local customs. But my experience is that, as a general rule, when volunteering outside of your camp or other lodging, women should cover their shoulders (no spaghetti straps), and wear dresses or skirts that are knee-to floor-length, with no slits extending above the knee. Capri pants for women may be acceptable in some areas. This is important to the village women, who have told me they do not want their men looking at visitors' legs and bare shoulders. Men should wear pants unless local dress allows for shorts. Be culturally sensitive regarding any pictures or words that are emblazoned across any shirts you wear.

The sun can be quite hot. Bring good sunglasses and a hat. You will likely need sunscreen. A rain jacket comes in handy if you travel during the wet season. The rains can be sudden and torrential. Check to see if you need to bring your own towel. If yes, pack a quick-drying microfiber travel towel. As for shoes, sneakers or other close-toed shoes and good sandals work most often. My friend swears by "Crocs with socks." You do not want dirt-dwelling jiggers embedding in your hands and feet. Several volunteers have experienced the pain of having these flea sacs extracted with a sharp object like a needle.

Many insects inhabit Africa. While the malaria-carrying mosquito is commonly discussed as a potential health hazard, the bite from a tsetse fly may also be mentioned when you visit one of the national parks. African locals have shared that these flies may, but rarely do, transmit African sleeping sickness; however, the bite is very painful. Team members traveling to tsetse-infected areas should wear long-sleeved shirts and long pants. Neutral clothing colors such as khaki were also suggested, as the flies appear to be attracted to bright and dark colors, and especially blue.

Celebrating the Spirit of a Champion

Students of all ages love a day of Olympic sporting events. This time spent with the children is not about winning. It is about the concept that embodies the Olympic spirit and creed. Make Olympic rings out of white paper plates the students color. Teach about the history of the Olympics, and especially about sports in which the students' own country participates. They enjoy learning miscellaneous facts, such as how the actual distance of a marathon was determined. Allow them time to create pictures of their own Olympic mascot that represents their school.

A three-legged race is a great way to teach the advantages of working together. Use old neckties to bind one leg each from a pair of students as they race toward a goal, and they will quickly learn cooperation is the key to not falling down. Give three students at a time a golf ball on a wooden spoon with instructions to race to the finish line. This is more commonly known as the egg-and-spoon race; however, in schools with little food supplies, a golf ball is a much better choice. Dribbling soccer balls around cones is always great fun. "Jump the River," using the name of the country's closest or most famous river is very enjoyable for the students. Set two long ropes parallel to each other and as the children jump over them, continue to move them farther and farther apart. If anyone falls into the river by not making the jump over both ropes, they take a seat while the others continue jumping. Some students easily jump several feet. This event is where you hear the loudest cheering with each set of progressive jumps.

One of the best sports to add to an Olympic day is golf. Pack a few clubs and plastic golf balls in a long duffel bag. Children as well as their teachers are fascinated with the opportunity to hit a few balls toward a handmade flag.

At one school, preparation for the national school exam was a time of intense study for the students. They seemed to tire easily and lose focus. The teachers said if any student attended all of the tutoring classes and fully engaged in the classwork, at the end of each week, they could play golf during the afternoon hours. The students responded by faithfully showing up for class and participating in all of the lessons. Golf was a great motivator. They learned about how different swings result in different outcomes and why the clubs have different shapes and faces. And it never gets tiring seeing the expression on anyone's face, including my own, when a ball is whiffed. This is all-around good fun.

Adding a hydration/rest station to your Olympic sports rotation is always a good idea, especially on very hot days. Use poster board illustrations to teach the children about the ways water nourishes our bodies, how to minimize dehydration headaches, and why it is important to stay hydrated, especially so while actively participating in sports. Then provide each of them with a large serving of water. I found this short lesson to be a very simple yet effective teaching tool.

This poem is an example of the children's enthusiasm for sports:

Football
(*written by a boy, age 15*)

Football! Football! Football!
It has spread all over the world in recent years.
It is one of the most interesting games that I have ever watched and played.
In America, Europe, Africa, Asia, South America, and Australia,
It is almost like a "language" that is understood by everyone.
Some people call it soccer (in America),
While others still know it as Football.
Pass! Pass! Pass!
The ball flies on the ground of the football field,
Goals are scored, the people celebrate.
Look at the big names in the game of football!
David Beckam, Lionel Messi, Thierry Henry, Cristiano Ronaldo
Robinho, Kaka, Ronaldinho, Donovan,
Iniesta, Xavi, Dempsey, Drogba, Yaya Toure,
All names so well known in the world of football.
Such an interesting sport.
Let's enjoy the game!

I'm Coming Home

Volunteer trips affect people in different ways. For some, reentry to their lives at home is relatively easy. Others struggle with what they have witnessed and the disparities they encounter. When I returned home from my first African trip, I struggled with opening my refrigerator and seeing such an abundance of food, knowing the people I just left had little food of any kind. Thanksgiving was two days later, and I wrestled even more with the enormous amount of food on my table. I made a big mistake thinking I should start my Christmas shopping on Black Friday that year.

As I watched two women argue over the last cashmere sweater on a "daily special" table, I burst into tears over the fact that they were angrily fighting over a sweater when I had just met people who owned but one set of clothing. The women looked at me with great confusion, for they could not fathom my hidden turmoil.

If you struggle with reentry, seek people who have had similar experiences as yours. Talk through your emotions and share your difficulties with the transition. Remember that those around you have not changed; you are the one who may have changed. Absorb the experience. Embrace the change.

In the Driver's Seat

When driving in Africa, you will likely find some very good major roads and highways. In the remote areas, travel may be much more difficult. You may experience very dusty conditions or the need to frequently navigate very large potholes and ruts. When driving through a stretch of road with a friend whose homeland is in Africa, I noted she was expertly swerving from one side to the other due to the poor road conditions. She said, "You know in your country when someone is driving all over the road, swerving back and forth, and you think he is probably drunk or otherwise impaired? Well, in my country, when you are driving on these roads, if you are not swerving all over the place, then we think you are drunk or otherwise impaired."

If you plan to drive a vehicle in Africa, always precheck the country's driving requirements and rules. An international driving license may be needed. Some African countries drive on the right side of the road, some on the left. Also be on alert for wildlife when driving. Once our African project manager needed to be hospitalized when the vehicle he was driving was slammed on the driver's side by a kudu (antelope), which was being chased by a lion. I have also seen vehicles which unexpectedly have seemly irreparable mechanical repairs. But I have learned that duct tape works quite well in fixing a ruptured pipe or leak. It also allowed our truck to keep moving when the entire drive-shaft pulled out of the floor boards. Duct tape is a good thing to always carry in your backpack.

And in less rural areas, if you stop for directions and someone tells you to turn at the "robot," they are referring to the traffic light.

Tiny Bits of Wisdom

As a new volunteer, many experiences caught me off guard and I did not always know the appropriate way to react or the best response to make. In time, I learned more about what was cultural, what was resourceful, and how to balance the joy with the sorrow. The following are a few tidbits that experience taught me.

Shoestrings will likely be removed from donated shoes and used instead to hold up boys' pants that are too big for them. That is perfectly fine and a good use of resources.

When you distribute donated shoes, often when you return the following year, the tops of those shoes will be cut off to accommodate the growth of the children's feet. Again, this is good maximizing of available assets.

When distributing shoe donations to large groups, rather than creating chaos by having each individual try on shoes until one fits, instead use the wrist to elbow rule. For most people, the length of your forearm (from the crook of your elbow to your wrist) is about the same as length of your foot. Place a shoe there to see if it is the correct size.

Cures come in all forms, and often not with a pill. Sometimes sunglasses, a baseball cap, and a large cup of water can cure a young boy's frequent headaches. Always listen intently and with sincere empathy.

"African time" is not driven by a clock. This more relaxed attitude toward time might make pinpointing start times for meetings and projects a bit more difficult. You may find yourself in a polychronic culture, one in which people need to manage more than one thing at a time rather than in a strict sequence. One-hour waiting delays are not uncommon. Mothers need to collect water, prepare their children for school, and complete many other tasks before they can join extraneous events. This is where volunteers need to practice patience and understanding and find ways to work around the time. Work with their needs, not your expectations.

Jumping rope in hot sand in scorching temperatures to show children how good I used to be at that sport twenty years ago is not something that

I should do at my age. Know your limitations and behave accordingly, especially if good medical care is a long distance away. When engaging in a physical sport with the children, remember to drink enough water to stay hydrated. Dehydration can leave you feeling quite ill. Do not wait until you feel thirsty to drink water.

One of the very best gifts you can impart to the children you meet on your trip, and one of the very best gifts you can give to yourself, is spending quality time with the children. Play games like "Duck, Duck, Goose" and delight in their laughter. Teach them a song and let them teach you one too. Let them help you to build a basic swing and secure it to a tall tree. Watch them excitedly line up for a turn to "fly high in the air." Show them how to make a frisbee a flying disk and delight in watching them jump and leap for catches. Read a book to them and add your own enthusiastic animation to it. Hold their hands when they reach for yours.

Adhesive bandages heal wounds which cannot be seen. If a child patiently waits in line for more than an hour or two at your first-aid clinic, then approaches you with no visible wound or cut in the area in which he is pointing, just place a bandage there and give him a hug. That child's smile and jump for joy as he runs away to show his friends demonstrates the healing power of that small gesture.

If you hire a local driver, at some point he may ask you if you need a short call or a long call. He is not referencing anything related to your phone. He is asking if you need a bathroom break, and if yes, how much time he should allot for that. The first time that I experienced this, I could not fathom why he was concerned about my ability to make phone calls. It wasn't until he stopped for a "short call" himself and asked me to stay with the vehicle's possessions that I understood the phrase. If your travel is long in duration, understanding the ask might make that time more physically comfortable.

I have met many village children with the first name of Peace, Joy, Blessing, Faith, Angel, Goodness, Blessed, Precious, or Gift. Their mamas tell me each child is a blessing packaged by God, and that is reflected in the naming process. The mothers will look for your reaction. Sincerely tell them that the names and their children are beautiful. Their smiles of appreciation will warm your heart too.

Once we distributed bottles of juice and shampoo to a village school. The head mistress had requested this type of supply distribution, and she and the teachers were on hand to assist. Although these items were distributed in different lines, we had not taken the time to explain the difference to the children. Seeing a child spit out shampoo as small bubbles escaped from between his lips was not the desired outcome. When distributing donations, be sure to first explain what you are distributing and its purpose. Do not just assume that everyone understands your intent. Be especially carefully when distributing supplies to children.

I have often been asked if I feel safe on my journeys to African villages. Once, when I was coordinating a first-aid clinic, I walked by a large bush with very sharp edges on its leaves. One of the leaves sliced my upper arm, causing it to bleed. Immediately the teacher who accompanied me as my interpreter pulled out a knife and promptly severed that entire shoot of the bush. I asked him why he did that. He replied, "Because it hurt you. We cannot allow that to happen." So yes, I feel quite safe.

Children love to dance. Bring some good and appropriate music with you and let the dancing begin. Or better yet, ask the children to provide the music. One of the best dance songs that I have ever heard was created by children melodically tapping on empty discarded glass bottles using thick wooden sticks, others pounding out strong beats on handmade Africa drums or even just empty plastic yellow water containers, and a few others making really cool sounds by vocal percussion. I was not born blessed with the gift of being a good dancer. But when I join in the circle of dance, I dance like no one is watching. And it is a joyous feeling to be held in that community embrace. When adult women reach out their hands to invite you into their circle of dance, always accept the gift of inclusion. Sometimes a woman will remove her long waist scarf and tie it around your waist. You are then expected to shake your hips as you join the circle. Allow yourself to be woven into this fabric of African life. I am not a good hip shaker, certainly not even close to the African women who I have met, but this is all about just trying. Your effort will be appreciated. But remember to return the scarf at the end of the dance, for it is a temporary adornment.

Crafts can provide a tremendous opening into deep conversation. One of my favorite crafts is called the Super Circle Paper Mobile. Colorful heavyweight paper (use four of five different bright colors) is cut into 100-150 circles or other round shapes like a scalloped flower (more easily done if you use a two-inch paper punch). Provide colorful markers and ask the children to draw things that are important to them on each circle. Alternatively, you can choose a focused theme (such as items that promote peace). Cut twelve strings of fishing line (12-15 inches each) and tightly tie them to a 10-inch wooden embroidery hoop. Starting at the top of one fishing line, glue two different circles together, with the fishing line sandwiched between them. Move about one-half an inch down the line and repeat. Continue that process for all of the lines. Then tie three long pieces of fishing line around a key ring and tie that to three spaced out parts at the top of the embroidery loop. You now have a beautiful colorful mobile.

This mobile is not just any craft. Once it is completed and hung on a tree or in a classroom, ask the children what they drew and why. Stories will be told about red hearts and figures representing the families that are loved. Tea cups may represent the morning breakfast for a girl. Sore bare feet may represent the long walk to school or a jigger infestation. Guns may represent the month-long military training class that some high schoolers attend, and it is a sign of peacekeeping. Mosquitos represent malaria. A goat, bananas, or mangos may represent the main food sources. A book may represent a yearning for higher learning. A car may represent a future dream. Religious symbols like a cross or church represent faith. An eye with a teardrop may represent the loss of a family member. You may see letters such as "HIV negative" written inside of a yellow sun. You may even see a depiction of yourself – as a new friend. These hand-drawn small pictures tell many stories about the lives of the artists, and they are an easy gateway to free-flowing conversations. Allow time to explore the meaning of these colorful expressions.

Another craft that appeals to children is to create a mirror flower garden on their school wall. Purchase strong glue (such as Gorilla glue) and small flat rimless mirrors of varying shapes at your local craft or hobby store. With the headmaster's permission, glue the mirrors to a wall on the school building, assuring the height coincides with the varying heights of the students. Then allow the children to paint flower petals around the mirrors, adding stems and leaves that extend below the petals. Then watch them excitedly move mirror to mirror to see their reflections. You can't help but smile as you watch them bloom.

Accepting an invitation to enter a village home comes with varying circumstances. Once I entered a home with a very smoky fire burning in a pit in the sand floor. This was a means to keep the family warm during the cool evening hours. The thick smoke triggered an asthma attack, and I spent hours trying to fully resolve the accompanying shortness of breath. Worse yet, I left my inhaler at our place of lodging, more than an hour's drive away and on a day when our work would not be completed in the village for many more hours, and our truck was in use elsewhere. Sometimes I have been invited into a hut without realizing that a personal request for assistance would be made, one that would directly benefit the one individual but not the larger community. Think about how you would handle situations like these.

In a different hut, I found the most immaculate environment, and a home embellished by true artistry. The hut was painted golden yellow using colored sand, then lined with circles of grey using charcoal, and white using plain sand. This was rubbed into the mud hut by hand. Chairs made of cement and colored black in the same manner actually emerged from the inside walls of the hut itself. Hardened sand storage shelves in decorative shapes lined the interior wall. The creativity and beauty were spectacular. The invitation to enter this home was simply to display its natural beauty.

Gifts from villagers are often what is most readily available to them, such as papayas, avocados, mangos, or pineapple. Sometimes athletically gifted boys will shimmy to the very top of a coconut tree just to present you with a fresh coconut treat. A live squawking chicken might be a bit difficult to handle, but gifts like these are heartfelt. Accept with gratitude.

On more than one occasion when I brought crayons and coloring books for the village toddlers as a means to entertain them while I taught a health class to their mothers, I met young children who did not know what a crayon is or how to use it. It was a joyous experience to cradle their little hands in mine as I taught them how to hold the crayon, then helped them to move it across the paper. Their smiles grew and their eyes widened in wonderment as they saw the colors appear. Soon they needed no guidance and became absorbed in creating their own masterpieces. Take the time to assure that any craft you distribute is one the children can readily learn how to use. Then watch them delight in exploring their creations.

Funding an outdoor square slab of cement is a good monetary investment at a village school, and even a twenty-foot-by-twenty-foot area will work well. This becomes a multipurpose gathering place and will be used for performances of singing and dancing, artwork (bring colored chalk then source local alternatives), geography lessons, hopscotch, jacks, and even chess matches.

Learn people's names. Names are connections to people's personalities and individualism. Learning and using someone's name is a sign of recognition of their importance to you, acknowledgement that they matter. My name is a very difficult one for many in African villages to pronounce. It often takes several attempts, and then writing it on paper, to be better understood. And sometimes I have difficulty understanding someone else's name. I once called a little boy Samwell, until I saw it in writing and understood that his name is Samuel. Take the time to get it right. This is an easy and respectful way to build strong connections. Sometimes just being present and making this connection is more important than doing.

Be prepared to speak or sing spontaneously. Many times our teams were greeted with joyous song. Then we were asked to sing a song in return. The first few times this happened, we just looked at each other and not one of us could think of a song to sing. One time we just silently ran possibilities through our heads until someone said, "How about London Bridges?" Not our best American team moment. Once a team member learned, then taught all of us, the words to the host country's national anthem. That was so well received. On a different trip, a team member taught herself a song that she sung in the village's native language. That was met with wild applause. I once told an elder that I am not very good at singing or dancing. He shared this African proverb with me: "If you can walk, you can dance. If you can talk, you can sing." There is unity in song sharing, so arrive with a few in mind.

If you are volunteering with a restorative program with people who have experienced great trauma, you may be asked to join them in their morning or evening chapel. Be open to that, regardless of your faith beliefs. When I participated in chapel with the girls, I closed my eyes and felt light coursing through my body as the girls sang their praises to God. Their singing and dancing were contagious, and I felt myself swept up in their playful renditions, wondering why I don't pray at home with such open abandon. I looked forward to the songs they taught me, "We surrender, we surrender, unto you ohhh Lord, we surrender, we surrender," and "Do you love your Jesus, deep down in your heart? Yes, I love my Jesus, deep down in my heart, Ooooohhhh deep, deep, deep down down, deep down in my heart…" I was bursting with my own joy at the blessing of spending time with these girls, not yet realizing that my own heart and soul were healing and growing through their energy and devotions.

When you attend church services, you may be asked to share your testimony with the congregation. Decide in advance who from your team will be the speaker. Once when I was asked to speak, I just shared off the top of my head, and it seemed to go fine. Then the pastor continued her teaching as an extension of what I had expressed. But then fifteen minutes later, to my great surprise, she again invited me to the front of the church to further expand on my thoughts. I was not so well prepared for a second session so soon. If spontaneously speaking before groups of people is not easy for you, give it some thought as you prepare for your journey. This kind of sharing is full of richness and joy.

Pack a headlamp or a flashlight. African night skies often shimmer with a multitude of bright shining stars. But in areas with no electricity, navigating the nights can be quite difficult. On nights with no stars, visibility can be to the end of your arm. While traveling in that darkness on my way to use the outdoor latrine, I have stepped on a snake as well as fire ants. Neither was a pleasant experience and neither contributed to a good night's sleep.

Remember that in rural areas, foods may be washed in water that may not be safe for a new traveler to consume. One common example is salad.

I recommend avoiding eating lettuce during your short-term volunteer trip as it may have been washed in water that could adversely affect your health. When I consume fresh fruits or vegetables, I try to wash them myself in safe drinking water and then peel off the outer layer. Fruits like bananas and mangos are a safe bet. Many times I have seen volunteers want to experience "street food," and many times I have seen them become quite ill several hours later. Choose your meals wisely and with advice from your country hosts.

Pack hand sanitizer for those times when clean running water is not available to wash your dirty hands before meals.

If you are volunteering in a rural area in which the people are in need of nutritional supplements, you quickly realize that bringing bottles of vitamins to distribute is not a sustainable intervention. Consider planting *moringa oleifera* trees, if the local community leaders are in agreement with that. The leaves provide vitamins A and C, calcium, protein, potassium and other essential nutrients. Leaves can be eaten fresh or dried. They can also be ground into powder to sprinkle on breakfast porridge or in tea. The tree's pods are also edible and are rich in vitamin C. Moringa seeds contain oil that can be used for cooking. The seeds can also be used as a natural way to purify water. The trees are drought resistant and usually bloom eight months after planting. Seeds or small saplings usually can be purchased at very low cost, often less than one US dollar. Demonstrate consuming the leaves yourself to build trust in using this as a supplement in the fight against malnutrition.

If you hear the word "Mzungu," the locals may be addressing you if you are light skinned. This word literally means a person who wanders without purpose; however, I see it used more frequently to describe a person from a foreign country who has light (white) skin. Usually the person using it, often a child, is just trying to get your attention, especially if he is trying to make a craft sale or other request. Most often no offense is meant. In some of the gift shops you will even find shirts that say "My name is not Mzungu."

While airport and hotel souvenirs most often have fixed prices, crafts in street vendor shops are often not visibly priced. You can decide if you are willing to pay the "Mzungu price" or negotiate. Usually, the more you buy, the better deal you can negotiate. If this is your first experience like this, remember that you are the amateur. And remember that your goal should be for both parties to agree on a mutually satisfactory price. Negotiate fairly.

When you earn the trust of those with whom you are working in the villages or refugee camps, they may share some deep personal experiences with you. That may involve terrible things such a rape, torture, seeing their family killed, and other atrocities. Listen, deeply and intently. That is all that you really need to do in that moment. Witness their resiliency. I met a girl who had endured significant heartbreak and many difficult ordeals in her young life. I asked her how she maintained the strength and hope that she exuded in spite of her suffering. Without pause, she replied, "I never lost faith that God would find me. And He did." These experiences are gifts – respect and treasure them.

In some circumstances, stepping back into the background and allowing your African friends to step into the forefront is the right thing so do. On one trip, I stayed with a dear African friend who opened her house to me. I hired a local driver for transportation to our project sites. Both are amazing, caring people. We all traveled to a very remote village in need of basic living supplies. Girls were married off at young ages because with no school building, education was not yet an option. Food resources were scarce. So we drove back to the nearest outdoor market and purchased items, including cabbage, rice, beans, vegetables, and juice. When we returned to the village, my host and our driver exited our vehicle and began organizing the distribution. They eagerly took the lead in helping their fellow countrymen and women. I could see how serving in this way was so very important to them. A quote that I heard Mohammed Ali say popped into my mind: "Service to others is the rent you pay for your room here on Earth." They were serving others, making life in this village located in their home country a little better than the day before. I was fortunate to be able to fund the food supplies. But I didn't need to be the one to head up the distribution. The best outcome is achieved when leadership empowers others to take ownership in a situation like this.

Transportation in some African countries is done by boda boda, a motorcycle taxi. Use caution if choosing this as your means of travel. The boda boda driver may not have a helmet for you to wear, or the passenger's helmet may not fit or have a chin strap due to repeated wear. If you are carrying a bag, keep it securely wedged between you and the driver. Once I witnessed a thief attempting to snatch a woman's shoulder bag as she rode as a passenger on a boda boda through a congested street, and he almost pulled both the driver and passenger off the bike and onto the ground. Many accidents have occurred to passengers using these motorbikes, and some of the injuries were quite serious. A hospital emergency doctor told me that motorcycle taxi accidents were by far the leading cause of admission to emergencies rooms in his country. Having said that, many people use this as their most economical and main transport. Just be aware of the risk and use caution.

Short-term volunteer trips have the potential to do more harm than good if not properly vetted and if established guidelines are not followed. Work with a nonprofit which has direct collaborative ties to leaders in the African community in which you want to volunteer. Look for groups with proven sustainability and long-term goals as well as social responsibility towards the community in which it is working. Do not assume that you know what that community needs based on your short time there. This is their home – you are a visitor. Work alongside the people in the village, being careful to not take paid jobs from them through your own good intentions. Avoid tours of orphanages that serve only as a feel-good moment for a visitor who is allowed to briefly hold a baby for a photo opportunity. Be aware that all of these children may not actually be orphans, and that the orphanage management may ask you for money. Use due diligence when deciding where and with whom you want to volunteer. Find organizations that walk the talk, with a compelling voice and a humble heart.

I always purchase volunteer travel insurance, paying less than $50 for a full year's coverage if travel is related to humanitarian work. The rates can vary greatly, as does the coverage. A quick internet search will provide you with good options. After volunteering in Zimbabwe, then flying home to New York via Johannesburg, South Africa, I found myself stranded in Johannesburg for several days. Hurricane Sandy had pummeled the American East Coast, forcing closure of the airports. The travel insurance activated with one quick phone call.

When I finally arrived in New York, I discovered that my car, which was parked in an airport offsite lot, had been partially submerged in dirty water from the storm. The interior was sopping wet and smelled like dead fish. Some people reminded me that "no good deed goes unpunished." But I say a soggy, smelly car at the end of a fulfilling African trip is just part of the journey.

Some travelers carry a credit card. Some places, especially remote villages, are not able to accept credit cards as currency. If your research indicates this form of payment is an option, and it's one you prefer to use, notify your card carrier of your itinerary about a week before you travel to avoid potential card freezes due to suspected fraud. Prepay many of your trip expenses in advance when possible.

Do not assume American dollars are accepted everywhere you travel. US currency in fifty or one hundred dollar bills, dated 2008 or newer, and with no markings of any kind, tend to exchange for the best rate in some East African countries. US banks will likely provide you with crisp new bills upon request if you explain the need. If you purchase items in rural craft markets, be sure to carry small bills in the correct currency to assist the crafters with easy exchange of their goods.

Tourist areas such as airports and hotels may inflate exchange rates, and therefore may not be the best option for the highest rate of return. When you exchange your country's currency at African banks, you may find varying exchange rates at different banks. Taking a bit of time to search for the best rate can increase your monetary return. These banks frequently post armed guards at the entrance door. Be respectful and comfortable with that sight.

Research how you might safely charge devices, such as your phone, laptop, and camera. You do not want to inadvertently fry your laptop. Power banks and solar chargers could be good options, depending on where you are traveling and how frequently you need to charge. Leave electrical devices like your hairdryer at home. In my experience with long hair in hot, humid environments, every day is a bad hair day, but that never really matters.

This next advice applies to any kind of travel, but is particularly important if you are traveling to an area in which the level of medical options is not equal to what you experience in your home environment – never pack your prescription medications in your checked luggage. Air travel is unpredictable, and you might find yourself without your needed medications. Once we stopped in a coastal African country to refuel, only to then be stranded in that country without our checked bags for another two days until a needed repair could be made to our plane. At the end of a different trip, we departed an African airport as the first leg of our journey back home, and about thirty minutes later, the pilot announced that we did not have enough fuel to fly to our first destination. We then needed to fly in the opposite direction to a different country to adequately fuel. This resulted in arrival at our layover destination too late to board our flight to the United States, thus necessitating an overnight stay without our checked luggage. On a different trip, a team member with a critical need for a liquid prescription medication packed her second glass bottle of that medication in her checked bag. The glass bottle broke during handling, and this medication was not available in the country in which we were volunteering. Always pack important and fragile items in your carry-on bag.

Also, pack a day's worth of clothes in your carry-on. If you are stranded for two or three days due to unexpected travel delays, you will welcome a change of clothes.

People often tell me to "Have a great vacation in Africa!" Somehow I need to find a better way to explain that this is never a vacation. You see great joy. But you also see death and hundreds of children in need who you want wrap in your arms, and to clothe and feed, and to protect. Your heart breaks, and then heals, only to break and heal again. You hope you are always growing in strength so that your heart never breaks and shatters. You grow in your own faith, as the people around you glow in their strong spirituality, sure of their path, and renewed with each sunrise, even if their road ahead is a rugged one. But these volunteer trips are not vacations, and understanding that is important before you embark on a journey like this.

When you look at pictures that a volunteer took on a humanitarian aid trip, look at what is going on in the background of each picture. You will see people helping or comforting each other in many different ways, women laughing, children playing with soccer balls made of banana leaves and twine, mothers feeding their children, dishes and laundry being washed by hand in a basin, fires being started in preparation for the evening meal, five- and six-year-old children carrying their siblings on their backs and lovingly caring for them, neighbors reaching out their hands to comfort someone who is suffering, aid workers trying to hide their tears, and so many other things that help you to step into life there. Often the forefront focus of the picture is not the actual story. The background reveals the real story. Often the photographer does not even realize that until someone asks a question while browsing through the photographs. Remember to not make yourself the focal point of your pictures.

In Africa, you find yourself constantly shedding tears – happy tears and sad tears, and often both on the same day. Those tears help you to open your heart and mind more and more to what you are experiencing, maybe for the first time. Crying makes us human. Transformation happens through the tears, as tears can transform our sadness into strength. It is OK to cry. Find your balance.

Children in Africa repeatedly ask me one very good question: Why do I only speak one language? I realized I am constantly asking people in Africa if they speak English. Often not only do they speak English, but they also speak at least one, and often two or three other languages. So why do I expect everyone else in the world to speak English just because I do? Why am I monolinguistic? Yes, they ask a very good question. I need to work on that. Before you travel, learn a few local phrases in the native African language. "Hello, how are you?" and "Thank you" are always ones good to know.

Even if you struggle with the correct way to say the words, the effort is greatly appreciated by your host community. Mistakes in pronunciation can lead to some good-natured bonding. Once I called a group of boys "little farts" when I was instead trying to say hello. They could not stop laughing. When my interpreter regained her own composure enough to explain what I had said to them, none of us could stop laughing. Another time I struggled with the difference in pronouncing amazzi and amazi, which sounded the same to me. Inadvertently, as I was teaching the menstrual pad project to a group of women, I inadvertently told them to wash their dirty cloth menstrual pads in amazi (feces) instead of amazzi (water). I knew from their shaking shoulders that they were trying to suppress laughter because I had missed the second "z" sound. And then we all laughed. They told me to keep trying to learn the language, as they appreciated the effort. After that, I learned to emphasize the second "z"!

Never promise a child that when you return home, you will sponsor him or her for school fees. Sponsorships should be fully vetted through responsible not-for-profit organizations already working in that village, or through other responsible means. Organizations who offer sponsorships likely have a standard way of assessing the need for sponsorships. But most importantly, your promise gives that child solid hope and great expectations. Crushing that hope by not delivering on your promise can be very damaging to these children.

Do not provide your personal phone number or email address to everyone who asks. The same applies to becoming "friends" on social media. If you allow that kind of personal connection during a short-term trip, be prepared for calls or emails once you return home, often asking for direct assistance. Those requests and the appropriate responses for handling them should always be vetted through the nonprofit organization with which you are working.

Some countries require your US passport to have a one or more blank pages to accommodate the entry and exit immigration stamps. Some visa stamps are large enough to cover a full page. Also note that the last two pages of your US passport are "endorsement" pages, and are not considered blank pages for visas. Some countries require that a passport be valid for at least six months before you travel. Verify country passport requirements prior to traveling. And check your passport expiration date well in advance of your trip.

Make a copy of your passport and travel arrangements, and leave those with a trusted person before you depart on your African journey.

Carry a copy of your passport with you. If possible, leave your original passport in a safe place once you arrive at your destination, and carry the copy with you.

Educate yourself about the visa requirements and fees related to the country in which you plan to travel. Sometimes you pay with a crisp new bill at the point of entry. Sometimes you must complete the online application and pay the fee prior to your trip. The visa fees vary by country.

Some countries require a yellow fever vaccination for entry, unless you have a signed medical practitioner vaccination medical waiver. Be sure to verify that and carry your yellow card as proof of vaccination. Vaccinations for hepatitis A and B are often recommended. Research the need for any additional vaccinations, and allow yourself plenty of time for this step as some vaccinations are given as a series of shots months apart. Discuss malaria prophylaxis with your primary care physician or travel practitioner. Several options exist and they each carry the potential for different side effects, including sleep disturbances such as insomnia and vivid dreams, and contraindications, including psychiatric reactions such as depression and anxiety. It is important to tell your physician about any health conditions, including any mild depression. An example of a more recent added concern is the coronavirus pandemic, which ushered in its own set of travel restrictions. Check travel requirements for all stages of your trip.

When carrying your cell phone, use extra care in places like a pit latrine. I have seen more than one volunteer standing in anguish after accidentally dropping their cell phone down a thirteen-foot toilet pit.

Before you dive into any African lake, be sure to ask about the hazards. The lakes are often quite beautiful and seemingly clean. Yet they can harbor parasites which can make you quite ill. Crocodiles and hippopotamuses can be found in rivers, and initially can be difficult to spot. Both are dangerous to humans. Check with the locals before you swim or bungee jump. If you embark on a riverboat tour and the local tour guide advises you to always keep your hands and feet inside the boat at all times, heed that advice. This may seem like obvious advice; however, I have seen volunteers tempting fate in these situations. Choose caution over living on the edge when engaging in potentially hazardous situations.

When you make a strong connection with someone who you met on your trip, you may think about funding that person's journey to visit you in your own home. Think that through very carefully and ask yourself all of the whys. If this becomes your vision of seeing your guest see his first movie or her first trip to your abundantly stocked grocery store, or of sharing your material ways of life with him, reconsider your plan. I have seen many well-meaning volunteers do this, then watched the fallout. Sometimes your guest decides that he wants to stay with you and not return home. Sometimes too much exposure too fast makes it difficult for her to contently return to her own home. Sometimes he becomes overcome by life here and requests to return to his home before the scheduled flight.

One such guest was appalled by schoolchildren tossing pens or pencils in the garbage because they did not like the way they felt in their hands, and by observing people ordering large amounts of restaurant food and not consuming it all, leaving it for waste disposal. His village was in desperate need of school supplies and food. While this may have been the norm at the volunteer's home community, these acts were perceived as very offensive by the African guest. He just wanted to return home. Be sure to take the time to consider the logistics and purpose of this kind of invitation to minimize any harm.

epilogue

When traveling to volunteer, always remember that you are there to embrace the culture, not to replace it. This is very important so as to not start thinking that you are the hero, there to only impart your ways, because your ways are better. Some people refer to that as the savior complex. Take the time to learn and listen from the locals. Stay humble. Always be respectful. Sometimes I have heard team members telling stories about their trip, make laughing references to the need to use an outdoor pit latrine. Think about that before you do so. This is a normal way of life in many villages. And it is perfectly fine. I grew up without a bathroom in our American house, and we used an outhouse. Honor what you see and appropriately reflect that in your post-trip storytelling. Those stories are a window to others and one that also reflects your own character and integrity.

As much as I yearn to at times, I cannot save everyone from all things bad. And that realization should not stop me from trying to help people continue to grow the good that is already in place. All I need to do is try my very best and, with a pure heart, to give love and encouragement, and to remember that no one needs my pity, but that people deserve my full respect. With that, maybe I can help the people who I touch in some small way. In turn, they help me to be a much better person, and one who continues to learn more about community, faith, hope, and the goodness that exists in this big world that we all share. And one who is always learning to dance in the light.

My eyes continue to be opened. I cannot unsee what I saw. I cannot unhear what I heard. Nor do I want to unsee or unhear. I am blessed, not a blessing.

In my years of volunteering in Africa, I have experienced so much joy and laughter. I have also cried more tears than I thought possible. And yes, it has all been worth it.

Lastly, and most importantly, I need to always remember that I need Africa more than Africa needs me. I find such great joy in sharing time and space with these resilient men and women and resourceful children, all of us working and playing together for a common purpose. A wise old man in a remote village asked me if I knew of a man from Austria named Viktor Frankel, who was a Holocaust survivor. He explained that he lived by this quote attributed to Frankel, "Everything can be taken from a man but one thing: the last of the human freedom – to choose one's attitude in any given set of circumstances, to choose one's own way." Prepare to meet amazing, beautiful people who will enrich your life in countless ways. Spend time with the elders. Spend time with the youth. Spend time just inhaling all that is Africa. When you exhale, you might just see the world a little more clearly and in a way that helps you decide how to wisely choose your own way, your own path. Then, with confidence and the right attitude, choose your own path. New adventures await. When you return home, return with the most valuable souvenir – your own personal stories. Be the voice of those who have no voice.

acknowledgements

I am abundantly grateful to the people in Africa who so warmly welcomed me into their world and who shared their stories with me. They have instilled within me a great love of African culture, its people, and their indominable spirit.

To friends and family who have supported my trips to Africa in so many ways, I extend my deepest appreciation. Your support allowed me to accomplish more than I ever could have initially imagined.

Special thanks to my Ugandan friend Bridget Nandawula, whose vibrant beauty graces the cover of this book.

These experiences, and subsequently the publication of this book, would not have been possible without the encouraging and compassionate support of my husband, Gregory. Your solid commitment to your faith, family, and friends has been such a bright light in my life. Thank you for being magnificent you.